A Brief History of
Heresy

Blackwell Brief Histories of
Religion

This series offers brief, accessible and lively accounts of key topics within theology and religion. Each volume presents both academic and general readers with a selected history of topics which have had a profound effect on religious and cultural life. The word "history" is, therefore, understood in its broadest cultural and social sense. The volumes are based on serious scholarship but they are written engagingly and in terms readily understood by general readers.

Published

Alister E. McGrath – A Brief History of Heaven
G. R. Evans – A Brief History of Heresy

Forthcoming

Carter Lindberg – A Brief History of Love
Douglas Davies – A Brief History of Death
Dana Robert – A Brief History of Mission
Tamara Sonn – A Brief History of Islam

A Brief History of

Heresy

G. R. EVANS

Blackwell
Publishing

350 Main Street, Malden, MA 02148-5020, USA
108 Cowley Road, Oxford OX4 1JF, UK
550 Swanston Street, Carlton, Victoria 3053, Australia

First published 2003 by Blackwell Publishing Ltd
Reprinted 2004

Library of Congress Cataloging-in-Publication Data
  Evans, G. R. (Gillian Rosemary)
    A brief history of heresy / G. R. Evans.
      p. cm. – (Blackwell brief histories of religion)
    Includes bibliographical references and index.
      ISBN 0-631-23525-6 (alk. paper) – ISBN 0-631-23526-4 (pbk. : alk.
  paper)
  1. Heresy–History. I. Title. II. Series.
  BT1315.3 .E93 2002
  273–dc21   2002007334

A catalogue record for this title is available from the British Library.

Set in 9.5/12pt Meridian by Graphicraft Limited, Hong Kong
Printed and bound in the United Kingdom
by TJ International, Padstow, Cornwall

For further information on
Blackwell Publishing, visit our website:
http://www.blackwellpublishing.com

Contents

List of Illustrations

Picture research by Charlotte Morris.

Preface

The extreme fundamentalism which has manifested itself so disquietingly in other religions in recent years with devastating global effect, has had its counterparts through-out Christian history, in religious wars and the persecution of individuals and groups of dissidents. This is a book about 'heresy' in Christianity, where the issues are distinctive because it is of the essence of Christianity that there be agreement in a common faith. Or so everyone thought for many centuries. The modern opening up of that fundamental assumption to active questioning makes a book like this topical, and perhaps a useful aid to those engaged in inter-faith and ecumenical conversations as well as those conscious of living in a predominantly secular society where Christians are one of a number of 'faith communities'.

The Christian presumption has always been that life is lived in search of salvation. Some have thought that should be an active search, involving a positive effort; others have seen it as a gift of grace which cannot be deserved by trying. But both viewpoints take true faith to be central. The Christian who is striving to be good needs to be clear what 'being good' means. The Christian who simply trusts in Christ, as an act of 'justifying faith', must still have the true faith.

What is 'required', then? Is the test what the individual Christian believes? Is the test 'a justifying faith in Christ', not in the sense of the content of what is believed but in the sense of 'trust in him'? That was what Luther argued, pointing out that even devils have a knowledge of Christ. Is personal faith enough, or must the individual be a *member* of a 'community of faith'? Or are neither necessary if God can act directly (by 'grace'), choosing to 'save' some individuals to be with him in eternity, perhaps even without regard to their beliefs or their membership of the visible Church? The extreme fear of anything which seemed to undermine the unity and integrity of the faith manifested throughout most of the events described in this book is therefore a recognition of the immense significance of what is at stake.

The unity brought into question by the challenge of heresy has not only been of 'faith in one Christ', involving a particular set of 'beliefs about him'. It has also involved questions of 'order'. It has frequently been asserted that there is 'no salvation outside the Church': *nulla salus extra ecclesiam*. Yet order in the Church is something much deeper than structural unity. When the Church is visibly divided, with one worshipping community set against another, it is suffering a breakdown of unity in its 'order' just as much as when there is an 'invisible' loss of the sense of community and common purpose. We shall see throughout this book the two threads of heresy (where some persist in choosing to believe differently from others) and schism (where there is division on a point of order), intertwined at almost every point.

When Augustine of Hippo (354–430) said that not every error is heresy, he was saying something almost universally agreed in Christian history.[1] The Spanish theologian Isidore of Seville (c.560–636) explains that the Greek *haeresis* carries the sense of making a choice. Heretics are those who 'holding perverse dogma, draw apart from the Church of their own free will'.[2] He includes similar themes in his *On Heresies*, though it covers fewer heresies than the *Etymologies* and discusses them more briefly.[3] In *On Heresies*, Isidore stresses that heretics are those who not only think wrongly, but persist with determined wickedness (*pertinaci pravitate*) in thinking wrongly.[4] It is important that they are exercising free choice when they opt for the wrong opinions; their fault is moral as well as intellectual. By contrast, an *orthodoxus* is 'a man upright in faith' who is also living a good Christian life.[5]

Isidore tried to explain the difference between the Church and the 'sects'. He explains that it is a mark of the true Church that it is not, 'like the conventicles of the heretics', in huddles in different regions, but spread throughout all the world,[6] so that the same Church is to be found in every place. 'Huddles' are exactly what we shall see, in succeeding centuries, as groups of 'outlaws' from the faith meet secretly in one another's houses.

There is no heresy which is not attacked by other heretics, says Bede (c.673–735).[7] Historically, as well as theologically, this has proved to be true. For once a group has set itself apart, or been officially cast off by the Church, it has often fragmented in its turn. Yet the fragments fall into patterns. These patterns and the favourite themes of heresy which we shall see repeating in the following pages give this book its natural shape.

Clusters of heretical beliefs aggregate in every century, or it seems to contemporaries that they do. The controversial Bohemian Jan Hus in the early fifteenth century tried to give the picture in outline.

There are three kinds of heresy according to the most famous doctors: namely, simony, blasphemy, and apostasy which, though not in reality distinguishable as opposites, yet are nevertheless distinguished as to cause. Apostasy consists generally . . . of man's deviation from the religion of God; blasphemy is . . . man's calumny of God's power; but simony consists, according to reason, in man's destroying altogether God's ordinances.[8]

For all these reasons it is not an easy task to give a tidy account now of the ways in which heretical opinions clustered together in reality. The considerable surviving literature is mostly the work of those trying to change the minds of heretics. They had their own agendas about the ways in which they presented the ideas they were challenging. The 'heretics' and 'schismatics' themselves would not necessarily recognize themselves in the descriptions of their critics.

There has been great nervousness about 'novelty' throughout the history of the Church. This has been taken to an extreme in the Orthodox Churches of the 'Eastern' half of the ancient Roman Empire, which became divided from the Western Church in stages, first (in the case of the Oriental Orthodox Churches) at the Council of Chalcedon in 451 and then (in the case of the Orthodox Church) with the schism which began in 1054, and which still divides the Orthodox Churches from the rest of the Christian world. The division was originally as much about politics as theology, but central to it was the accusation that the West had been 'adding things' to the Creed.

The Orthodox held with determination to the positions articulated in the first few centuries and they resisted any departure from, or development of, what could be said then, on the grounds that if it was new it could not be authentically part of the true faith. By the iconoclast era of the seventh to ninth century, the acts of their Councils tended to follow a standard format, reflecting the procedure which was used at the Council itself in the actual discussion. This was the time when one party wanted to destroy all the images of saints which were so much reverenced by ordinary people. Accounts of significant discussions of theological topics were preserved with care and recopied, even put into *florilegia* or collections of extracts, so that they could be referred to as disputes continued.[9] The Church in this part of the world was trying hard to ensure that it was faithful to the decisions of the Church of earlier times.

Even if it has not been such a central preoccupation there, in the West, too, there has been a consistent association of 'new' with 'wrong'. In the four short books he wrote against the heretics at the end of the twelfth century, Alan of Lille identifies 'new' heresies among the 'old heresies' which are themselves still unacceptable because of their novelty, even if they are familiar. Among the 'very new' or 'newest' heresies the heretics of his own day are, he says, disporting themselves like drunken men. They have gone beyond their predecessors in that in former times the heretics erred merely in attempting to solve the deep problems of theology with the aid of human reason; these new heretics 'are restrained by neither human nor divine reason'; they devise monstrosities. Alan of Lille tries to get things back under control by using the arguments already devised against the former heresies when they were 'new', for they have acquired a certain established character over against these even newer departures from the true faith.[10]

The accusation of novelty has come from both 'sides'. It has not only been made by the 'official' Church against dissidents. Two centuries later, at the end of the fourteenth century, the dissident John Wyclif (c.1329–84) was accusing the members of religious orders in his own day of introducing novelties without divine authority.[11] Wyclif explains that one of the Devil's devices has been to invent new notions which go against the law of Christ.[12] Wyclif mistrusted the religious orders of his day, particularly the friars, for their 'novelty'. They are 'newe mannys ordres', and therefore of human invention. That means that people are following human leaders instead of following Christ. It means they are adding to the teaching of Christ new 'requirements' for salvation. They also bring in a form of slavery, for they keep some out of orders to which others may belong. They require unnecessary 'observances' of human origin, such as the wearing of habits.

Yet some have recognized that there may be benefit in discussing the 'heretical' ideas which are bound to arise in every generation. It is a good defence against being led astray. Jan Hus, Wyclif's younger Bohemian contemporary, was robust in his attitude to teachings which seemed 'risky'. He thought there was value in reading and discussing heretical ideas, for something was often to be learned from them. In his *On Reading the Books of Heretics*, a work which made the Archbishop angry and still more determined to bring him to justice, Hus cited St. Paul's view that 'it was right that there should be heretics' (1 Corinthians 11.19). The Church needs to encounter such tests in order to learn where the truth lies. 'The books of the heretics are to be read, not burned, so long as there is truth in what they say' (*dum in ipsis veritas continetur*). They can, he points out, often be supported by the authority of the Fathers, by canon law or by reason.[13] The books of the heretics, he says, have the capacity to stir up spirituality, to clarify the truth, and, paradoxically, to encourage the reader to seek the truth so as to avoid falling into the same errors. He cites Augustine on this point.[14] Hus did not hesitate to point out that the Church itself over the centuries had had to 'correct', or 'expressly revoke' many things which it had allowed to appear in its teaching. Similarly, the most respected authors had had their periods of condemnation. Peter Lombard's *Sentences* was criticized at first on many points, but far from being burned it had now become a standard work.[15]

Jan Hus was probably right, but even if he was mistaken in urging the usefulness of discussing dissenting opinions and differences of view, he was noting something which has happened throughout Christian history. Even a *Brief History of Heresy* is a dip into forbidden territory.

Chapter 1

The Importance of Being United

The outward reasons why the Christian Church has wanted to be united have changed over the centuries. The deeper reasons have had the same inner coherence in every century. At the beginning it was essential for Christianity to make itself distinct from Judaism and from contemporary polytheistic pagan religions. As the young Church grew in numbers and evolved a more complex structure, there were also practical problems to do with keeping control over change and development, so that the Christian faith would not fragment into a thousand different forms.

These were considerations about the community. For many Christians in the modern Western world the relationship of the individual soul with God seems all-important. But this is a comparatively recent emphasis. It was brought to the forefront of believers' minds by the debates of the sixteenth century and after in the West, which created the churches of the Reformation. First there were moves away from the insistence on the universality or catholicity of the Church. Many Reformation leaders rejected the 'visible' universal Church of the day as corrupted by Antichrist and claimed that the true Church was invisible and known only to God. Others pointed to a visible church of their own adherents as the true Church.

Then there was a diminution of the sense of community. Pietism and the Enlightenment of the eighteenth century encouraged the faithful to believe that what mattered was personal commitment rather than (and not as well as) membership of the community of a 'visible' universal Church.

The early Christian picture was quite different. Christians, following Christ's command, left their fathers and their mothers and went out to preach the Gospel. They won disciples. The stress was on the building up of a 'community' of followers of Christ, the body of which he was the Head. This is the Church (with a capital C) in the sense in which the term is mainly used in this book. With a small 'c', 'church' is used here for the local community or sometimes the divided community, for something which is not that complete single *koinonia* (the New Testament term for 'community' in the particular form it took in the Church). It became obvious early on that the human reality did not always match the ideal, and that even in individual localities the churches were internally divided. But that did not diminish the importance of the ideal of unity.

'Being one' in this way was a strong theme in Christianity from the beginning. 'Though we are many, we are one body in union with Christ, and we are all joined to each other as different parts of one body' (Romans 12.5). On this understanding that it is a religion of 'community', Christianity makes sense only if it expresses itself in unity, and at the beginning it was natural to see this as a 'visible' unity. By baptism Christians become members of this 'body' which 'is the Church'. St Paul emphasizes that this is 'one baptism', by which 'Christians have been baptized into the one body' (1 Corinthians 12.13).

One central reason why has it been regarded as so important in the history of Christianity that there should be 'one faith' is that the faith in question was 'faith in Christ', an expression of this 'unity with Christ himself'. He himself underlined the point and made it central at the Last Supper he ate with his disciples before he was crucified. He took bread and said 'This is my body', before breaking it and sharing it with his disciples. 'The bread we break, when we eat it, we are sharing in the body of Christ', said Paul in his first letter to the Christians at Corinth (1 Corinthians 10.17). That is why the Eucharist he instituted is also known as Holy Communion.

The context of worship is important. The early Christian community met in worship. Its members prayed to Jesus as Lord, as no Jewish community could do. The Jews insisted that the God of Abraham, Isaac and Jacob was one God and unless Jesus was clearly understood to be himself God they could not call Jesus 'Lord' in worship. To baptize in the name of Father, Son and Holy Spirit required explanation and clarification. That explanation and others like it, particularly about the relationship of this Jesus to humanity, had to be forthcoming again and again as the first Christians spread the Gospel among Jews and those of other religions. So liturgical and missionary contexts actively helped to shape the understanding of the faith and to set the main parameters of its orthodoxy.

The expectation was strong at the beginning that very soon the community of Jesus's disciples would be with him in heaven, enjoying for eternity a 'communion' or 'fellowship' (*koinonia*) of the perfect love of God and love of one's neighbour (Mark 12.31). This urgent sense of the importance of keeping the flock together and ready has manifested itself afresh repeatedly throughout Christian history, whenever – as has happened again and again – there have been fears that the end of the world was imminent.

In such heightened periods of anxiety, it has been easy to see heresy and schism as having a cosmic significance, as part of a Satanic plot against God. Filastrius, author of the *acta* of the Council of Aquileia in 381, wrote a *Book on Divers Heresies*, in which he places the origin of the plague (*pestilentia*) of these heresies in the events at the beginning of the world, when Adam sinned, and he blames first the Jews for its diffusion, and later the idolatry of Christians.[1]

But at a much more workaday level there have emerged repeating patterns of dissident and divisive opinion. Schleiermacher, in the nineteenth century, saw heresy as that which defines human nature or Christ as the redeemer in such a way that redemption cannot be accomplished.[2] He thought that by his own time the repeating patterns could no longer easily be reduced to a simple alternative, an antithesis of Catholic and heretical: 'We must rather start from the essence of Christianity, and seek to construe the heretical in its manifold forms by asking in how many different ways the essence of Christianity can be contradicted, and the appearance of Christianity yet remain'.[3] He breaks down the patterns into broad types, many of which which will be recognizable in the story which is told in this book. Schleiermacher's idea was that some (for example, the Docetists) have gone 'astray' by seeing Christ as a pretence, not really human and so not bringing about a 'real' redemption; others have made the mistake of seeing Christ as a mere example, to be imitated, which has removed his power to redeem; others, such as the Manichees and other dualists, have seen humanity as fundamentally tainted by evil from its very creation; a fourth group (the Pelagians and their like) have made the opposite mistake of considering humanity to be essentially good and therefore capable of perfecting itself by effort.[4] This reading is not necessarily in tune with all the stories to be found here, but it is a useful starting-point for the exercise of trying to see the underlying tendencies away from a balanced and consensual faith which have run away with individuals and groups of believers in certain directions again and again over the centuries.

Forming Consensus

In a Christian Church conceived from the beginning as a community bound by a shared faith and a shared personal commitment to Christ, how have some believers disagreed with the mainstream views about the faith or found themselves separated from the rest of the community?

The reality has usually been that there was no intention of separateness at the start. Someone has raised a question, often a question no one had thought of before. The early centuries of Christianity opened up a great many such questions in the ordinary course of people's attempts to live a 'Christian' life in imitation of Christ. As they set about following Christ's commandments daily decisions had to be made. Those who were Jews were accustomed to rules about not eating 'unclean' foods. Did those still apply? Were Christians still bound to obey all the other laws of the Old Testament? Was it necessary to be circumcised as well as baptized? Several such questions can be seen causing divisiveness in the Acts of the Apostles. Some of those who were preaching the Christian faith taught converts that they had to be circumcised in the traditional Jewish way if they were to become Christians. Others said that was completely unnecessary, for Christians were not bound by the old law.

These were questions which were not easily resolved, and which were to reappear over the centuries in groups whose opinions were episodically condemned by the Church. One way to understand the complex phenomenon of 'heresy' is to explore in this way how a particular idea or preoccupation resurfaces. For example, the 'Passagians' believed in literal obedience to the Law of the Old Testament. The Passagians were said to rely on the authority of the Lord speaking in Matthew: 'do not think that I am come to destroy the Law or the prophets. I am not come to destroy but to fulfil' (Matthew 5.17). There follows a series of further texts from Scripture, from each of which is drawn the conclusion, 'for this reason all things that are included in the law are to be observed'. These observances included requiring circumcision, strict Sabbath observance, strict observance of Old Testament dietary laws, but not 'ecclesiastical institutions which the heretics seek to annul entirely, calling them superfluous'.[5] The Passagians were condemned by the Pope in 1184 and there is no evidence that they survived long after his formal disapproval was made official, or that they were very widespread. Nevertheless their leading ideas were bound to be a continuing concern when it had not proved easy for the early Church to settle this question either.

One of the ramifications of this continuing debate about the place of the commandments of the Old Law in the new Christian dispensation is picked up by John Wyclif.[6] Does Scripture teach that it is necessary to obey the law in order to be saved, he asks? Recent heretics, claimed Wyclif, say that no one can obey the law perfectly, and if that is so, none can be saved. That must mean that there is no need to obey the law. This rather startling inference was intended to test the waters. Wyclif himself believed that there *is* an obligation on Christians to obey God's law, and that it is possible for everyone God intends to save to do so.[7]

This is even made into an argument in favour of the provision of vernacular versions of the texts in which the law is written, for everyone will need to know what the law is.[8] Some contemporaries insisted that it was necessary for at least the Ten Commandments to be available in English as well as in Latin. There had been some 'progress' on this front in the provision of manuals for the less well-educated clergy to use. Archbishop Pecham had held a Provincial Council at Lambeth in 1281 at which a plan of 'instruction for the laity' was drawn up. In 1425 it was translated into English at the instigation of the Bishop of Bath and Wells, who had it put in every church in the diocese.

Another leading late mediaeval dissident, Jan Hus (c.1369–1415), argues that, 'with reference to the *ceremonialia*', or ceremonial ritual duties laid on the Jewish people, the Old Law is buried by the New, so that as Augustine says, if anyone submitted to circumcision in the Jewish way he would be counted a heretic. Nevertheless, the parts of the Old Testament which contain the *ceremonialia* are not to be burned.[9] This line of argument seems to place Hus outside the 'fundamentalist' stream. It is not his position that everything in the Bible must be taken as it stands. He sees the Bible as a whole, in which the New Testament alters for the Christian some of what is taught in the Old. Nevertheless, he is clearly still preoccupied with these questions which were dividing the first Christians.

The young Church had tried to deal with this evidently important practical question by meeting in a prototype of what was eventually to become a 'Council' of the Church and seeking consensus. They then agreed to write an explanatory letter (Acts 15.23–9), which could be read aloud in churches. This said that Christians did not need to feel burdened with the obligation to keep the whole of the Old Law; they need observe only a few basic rules. They should not eat meat which had been offered to idols and they should keep clear of sexual immorality.

This policy of seeking consensus was not as straightforward as it looked, because in the enlarging Church, it soon began to raise the question of the authority of such collective decisions. A small local meeting might have every local Christian present and joining in the discussion. But if the local churches were to succeed in maintaining a common faith it was necessary to devise a formal structure to enable their leaders to meet and settle disagreements on their behalf. That meant deciding who the leaders were and what kind of leaders they were to be and whether they could 'bind' those who had chosen them, when they met as their representatives. And that raises the vexed question of 'ministry' which will be visible everywhere in this book as a cause of division.

In the history of the Church there has been a series of 'conciliar' pronouncements, or statements of official gatherings of the Church in the persons of its representatives, made on the understanding that when Christians gathered together in that way the Holy Spirit was also present and they could be sure of having divine guidance in reaching their conclusions. The same careful work in trying to establish continuity with the faith of the first Christians has had to be done again and again, as the old questions arose afresh in each generation. The first of these to attempt a comprehensive statement or faith or Creed was the Council of Nicaea in 325. A revised version of the Nicene Creed was agreed by the Council of Constantinople in 381.

At the Council of Chalcedon in 451 a definition of the faith was agreed. In sending it out, the assembled bishops took as a starting-point the words of Jesus: 'My peace I give you, my peace I leave to you' (John 14.27). They explained that 'the evil one never stops trying to smother the seeds of religion with his own tares and is for ever inventing some novelty or other against the truth', so Christ has prompted the calling together of a Council of the leaders of the Church. They were reassuring that the Council has 'driven off erroneous doctrines' by its 'collective resolution', and it has 'renewed the unerring creed of the Fathers'. It has done this, they said, by reaffirming the Creed of the Council of Nicaea in 325 and that of the Council of Constantinople in 381, which was, in its turn a reaffirmation and refinement of the Nicene Creed.[10] They went on to list the heretical ideas their restatement of the creed outlaws and to insist that 'since we have formulated these things with all possible accuracy and attention . . . no one is permitted to produce, or even to write down or compose, any other creed or to think of teach otherwise'. Anyone who attempted it was to be deposed if a cleric or anathematized if a lay person.[11] This was a comprehensive enough attempt to fortify the Church against a recurrence of these difficulties.

Yet conciliar statements have not always been the 'last word'. The *consensus fidelium*, the gradually emerging informal 'agreement' or 'sense' of the whole 'people of God', has sometimes led to revisions of opinion over time. In the sixteenth century, the Council of Trent (1545–63) insisted on keeping the Latin Vulgate and banning the use of vernacular versions of the Bible. By the middle of the twentieth century, in the aftermath of the Second Vatican Council there had been a reversal. Priests who wanted to go on using Latin were being condemned by a Church which would formerly have regarded them as loyal to its teaching. So it is not easy with hindsight to identify some positions confidently as 'orthodox', conforming in their thinking with the settled view of the continuing Christian community, and others as 'divergent', or 'unorthodox'. And the reappearance of unresolved questions about the need to obey the Old Law shows how hard some questions were to settle.

The Papacy

Alongside the evolution of a balance between 'official' or 'conciliar' pronouncements and the emergence of the 'consensus of the faithful' have run other ways of finding out what to believe when in doubt. One of the most important of these in the West has been the rise of the papacy as a source of definitive pronouncements. Christianity began in the period when Rome dominated the local world. It began to mature as a religion in a Roman Empire entering its decline. After the fall of Rome a vestige of Empire was recreated in the form of the 'Holy Roman Empire'. This was set up when Charlemagne was crowned in 800. It assumed that there was to be a continuing relationship between Emperor and Pope, although the maintenance of a balance of power was to prove a crucial difficulty. For a large part of the Middle Ages it was believed that the first Christian Emperor Constantine had made a 'Donation' to Pope Hadrian, conceding supremacy to the spiritual power. That this was a Carolingian forgery, an invented document created about the eighth century, did not become apparent for many centuries. (Spotting forgeries was never easy in the Middle Ages, if a document claimed to come from an ancient authority.)

In the time of Pope Gregory the Great (c.540–604), there was already significant rivalry between the heads of the ancient patriarchates of Jerusalem, Antioch, Alexandria, Constantinople and Rome over which should be primate, with Rome claiming supremacy because it was the see of Peter. For had not Christ called Peter the rock on whom he would found his Church (Matthew 16.18). The Eastern Patriarchs not only resented this claim to predominance; they also objected to the very idea of a universal primacy. The Eastern custom was to regard the patriarchates as autocephalous, which meant that they were bound to keep the same faith, but free to run their own affairs under their separate 'heads'.

In the late eleventh century Pope Gregory VII (1073–85) began to press for an enlargement of the papal claims to plenitude of power in the West, and for recognition of the supremacy of Church over state in the West. The role of the papacy now began to be an important element in this story of the processes by which the continuity of the faith was maintained and 'orthodoxy' defined. That led to several centuries of power struggles between Church and state, but it also encouraged an aggrandizement of papal claims to power within the Western Church itself (and indeed in the Church as a whole, since the Bishop of Rome continued to seek to be recognized as universal primate). Bernard of Clairvaux summarized the position in his book *On Consideration*, written as a manual of advice for Pope Eugenius III (d.1153). He explained that the Pope is supreme over all powers on earth, and subject only to the authority of heaven.

From this point, popes increasingly began to behave like monarchs of the Church, with consequent diminution of the authority accorded to the Council of Bishops. These internal tensions, and the corruptions perhaps inevitably consequent upon allowing the papacy to make this bid for personal power, were the cause of much of the disaffection we shall find among the 'anti-establishment' dissidents discussed in this book. They also pointed down the road to Reformation.

With the invention of printing, the appearance of the polemical reforming literature of the sixteenth century presented a new problem. This was no occasional treatise, but a barrage of informed challenge. A Luther or a Calvin could have an immense influence when books could be so widely copied and distributed. In the 1550s local tribunals of the Holy Office were already making lists of works which Catholics were forbidden to read. Pope Paul IV published an Index of Prohibited Books in 1559. The Index banned the works of Luther and those of earlier dissidents such as Jan Hus. It also forbade the reading of the work of humanists like Erasmus of Rotterdam. There were less controversial bannings; the Church had always disapproved of writings on magic and it was not new for the Church to disapprove of writings tending to encourage immorality. But this systematic listing of books for banning was without precedent. The Council of Trent approved the Index in 1564 and in 1571 the next Pope, Pius V, a former Grand Inquisitor, created a special 'Congregation of the Index'. The Congregation of the Index remained in existence until 1917 and the last edition of the Index appeared in 1948.

This was the negative side of a developing positive doctrine of the *magisterium* or teaching office of the Church. At the Fourth Lateran Council of 1215 the Church was described as *mater et magistra*, not only Mother but Teacher. This was a strong version of the ancient idea that the leaders of the community would meet from time to time to discuss questions arising about the definition of the faith. In the West it was increasingly understood that the Pope occupied a special place in the teaching structure; Papal infallibility was gradually accepted, although it did not receive formal definition until 1870. Then the First Vatican Council decreed that papal pronouncements made *ex cathedra* on matters of faith and morals were infallible, even if no Council approved them. That was the far end of one road by which the faith was, in intention, kept whole and unchanged.

The Bible in the Hands of Heretics

It is high time to look at the place of the Bible in this story. When a question is asked which seems to be challenging received opinion it is convenient to turn to written authority for answers. The most important written source in Christian history has been the Bible. Historically, Scripture's authority cannot easily be separated from that of the Church; for the Bible was itself a product of the early Church. The idea of a 'canon' of Scriptures accepted as possessing special authority is to be found in Old Testament times. By the middle of the second century the four Gospels and the 13 epistles of Paul had emerged from a literature which included other 'gospels' and letters. Between the end of the second century and the first decades of the third century these came to have the same sort of standing and weight as the Old Testament. There was some local variation. Some churches accepted writings such as the *Shepherd of Hermas* and the *Epistle of Barnabas*. Gradually, other books now in the New

Testament 'canon' won acceptance, although doubts hung over Hebrews, Revelation and some of the non-Pauline epistles into the late third or fourth centuries. It is not until the time of Athanasius (369) that the present 'canon' appears complete. This process of 'acceptance' is hard to trace and it is still much disputed exactly how the list was arrived at. It was, however, given 'official' approvals which can be pointed to with more confidence. For instance, in 382 a Council at Rome gave a list of more or less the modern contents of Scripture (including a small group of books from the Old Testament period now known as the Apocrypha, which have not been accepted by many Protestant churches). So it was the Church which 'filtered' and decided upon the inclusion of the various elements in the early Christian Scriptures which eventually made up the Bible.

It was accepted quite early that the books of Holy Scripture were divinely inspired and therefore of supreme authority. Jerome (c.342–420), making the fresh translation into Latin which came to be known as the Vulgate, raised the question whether his translation itself was to be regarded as inspired. He did not think it was. He made a clear distinction between what he was doing, and the 'direct dictation' of the Holy Spirit which was generally seen as the privilege of the Evangelists and the divine inspiration which the Prophets were believed to have enjoyed. This distinction became very blurred as the Vulgate was read and discussed century by century, for it was difficult not to treat the Latin text as 'real' Scripture, when it was the only text available to most scholars.

The difficulties of ensuring that the 'interpretation' of Scripture did not lead readers 'away' from its message did not grow less with the centuries. We shall meet them everywhere in this book. The Pope, writing to the Masters of the University of Oxford in the fourteenth century about the problem of Wyclif, flattered them on their 'familiarity with the Scriptures, in whose sea you navigate, by the gifts of God, with an auspicious oar', for Wyclif's own interpretations were feared to be leading the faithful astray.[12]

The saving power of the Bible ought, in the view of the mediaeval Church, to be mediated through its teaching authority by its ordained and therefore authorized ministers, with the approval of the local bishop. It is for priests to decide religious questions, says Bernard of Fontcaud.[13] He pointed out that Moses said to the elders of Israel when he went up alone to speak with God, 'Wait here until I return to you. You have Aaron and Hur with you. If any question arises, refer it to them' (Exodus 24.14). Bernard says that it is not proper for the laity to preach. They do not have the authority; they may lead the faithful astray. He is clear that women cannot preach.[14]

But that is not so 'safe' a teaching if the Church's authorized ministers have gone astray, or fail to do their duty as teachers. Wyclif speaks strongly about the neglect of the duty to preach on Scripture by the clergy and religious of his day. 'The false brothers and dumb priests ought to be ashamed to omit to defend the Law of God'. Their failure to do so brings ruin to the faithful.[15] As one author puts it in the thirteenth century, 'The clergy of the Roman Church, on whose behalf you speak, are perverse and live against God and when they speak of God their speech is blasphemy'.[16] The ecclesiastical authorities, once 'proved' fallible, cannot be relied upon as interpreters of Scripture.

When popular heretics tried to understand the Bible for themselves and even presumed to interpret it for others by preaching, they were implicitly challenging the assumption that the Church was the vessel of salvation and its approved teaching the only safe way for the believer to follow.

By the early thirteenth century, this question of the 'right way to use the Bible' was a prominent topic of debate. The twelfth century had seen the creation of a standard gloss or commentary, the *Glossa Ordinaria*, put together as a complex patchwork by scholars drawing on the commentaries of the Fathers and filling in the gaps. Uneducated or half-educated self-appointed preachers were ignoring all this work and setting themselves up as independent commentators. It was bound to seem a challenge to the Church. Heretics, far from being brought to salvation by the Word of God, are led to their perdition by even the texts of Scripture when they interpret them perversely, says the thirteenth-century apologist Durandus of Huesca in his book *Against the Manichees*, which he wrote with the zeal of a convert as a former Waldensian heretic turned Catholic.[17] He explains that it is not of course the sacred text itself, but the construction placed upon it, which does the spiritual harm.[18]

Wyclif's *On the Church* (1378) sets forth a revolutionary doctrine of the Church. The rejection of the visible Church of the day as authoritative in its teaching and ministry encourages him to take 'Scripture alone' to be the locus and source of all authority. He is assuming that legislation promulgated by popes is 'mannis law', that is, a merely 'human' law which does not have divine sanction. Wyclif thus began to question with remorseless persistence the rightful authority of a Church which seemed to be setting itself against the principles Jesus laid down for his disciples and whose ordained ministry – the 'authorized' officers – were frequently unworthy. It is not in dispute that there was widespread disquiet on this point. The very twelfth-century and early thirteenth-century councils we saw condemning heretics also made extensive comment on the unacceptable behaviour of many of the clergy. The 'unworthy minister' question had been resolved in the patristic period in favour of an acceptance that divine grace can work through even the most corrupt of ministers. Augustine explained that the unworthiness of a minister did not invalidate what he did, provided he was acting and teaching in the true faith. There were exceptions. The Donatists of north Africa in the time of Augustine were not persuaded that it was possible to accept ministers whose ordination they thought invalid because it had at some stage in the chain involved the laying on of hands by ministers who had abandoned the faith under persecution and returned to it. But for the most part this confidence that divine grace works regardless even through unworthy ministers, had been a more or less settled question. But it was becoming difficult not to return to it in the face of widespread outrage about the excesses of some of the higher clergy in the high Middle Ages and their neglect of their real duties.

Wyclif writes that no one can hold true 'dominion' over others, or over possessions, while in a state of mortal sin. He says that some think that if a priest leads an evil life, that may take from him the power to administer the sacraments.[19] Wycliffites wanted to see ministers chosen according to God's law and not at the behest of princes or for money.[20] The wrong people, chosen for the wrong reasons, may be subject to avarice and worldly love, given to simony and, above all, eager for power.[21]

While defect in an unworthy minister might be supplied by grace with reference to his sacramental functions, it did not follow, to the thinking of many of the dissident groups, that a corrupt priest could be an adequate minister of the Word. Wyclif, like the Waldensians, saw ministry as an office in which the ministry of the Word is the most important thing. The minister is the vicar of Christ in that he feeds the people with the Word which is Christ. So the preaching office is primary.

Wyclif gives a further definition of heresy in his *De fundatione sectarum*, which contains another shift that is important for our purposes. He tries to make 'spirit-led exegesis' the norm: 'Anyone who pertinaciously expounds the faith of Scripture other than as the Holy Spirit directs, is a heretic'.[22] He touches here on a theme which was to prove important in the Reformation debates. Once the *magisterium* of the Church is denied, it is necessary to identify an authority which can keep the private reader of Scripture on the right path. Anything else is mere personal opinion. Wyclif explains (speaking for himself) that:

> as far as those parts of Scripture are concerned of whose meaning we have a [mere] opinion or are humbly uncertain, we regard our sense as held *opinative* and we are always prepared to concede the 'catholic meaning', whether it is expressed by the Pope or by some friar or by a lay person or by a learned man'.[23]

But where Scripture seems to him to give a clear lead, Wyclif will not submit to the Church's teaching.

In his *On the Truth of Holy Scripture*[24] Wyclif regards the Bible as the repository of all truth and as inerrant. He urges Christians 'to believe steadily in the faith of Scripture, and not to believe any other source on any subject unless what it says is based on Scripture'.[25] Wyclif was not hostile to the Church of earlier times. In fact, it is one of his objections to the sects that they expound the Scripture in ways which have no precedent in the Fathers.[26]

Heretics who thought like this were separating the Bible and the Church, and taking the Bible to be the only safe and sufficient guide. Scripture is its own illumination.[27] 'That opinion of the Apostle is clear and needs no exposition'.[28] Surviving poems reflect the same idea: 'But Scripture says, and it is quite clear'.[29] This theory of 'self-evidency' implicitly assumes that the faithful, reading the Bible for themselves, will have the guidance of the Holy Spirit to ensure that they do not go astray, for it is the Spirit which makes its meaning 'clear'. The preface to Wyclif's collected sermons on the Sunday Gospels sets out the principles,[30] that God's teaching may be clearer and he himself as preacher may be of use as God's servant.

Towards the end of his life, Wyclif came close to embracing the doctrine of *sola scriptura*, which became fundamental to many of the reformers of the sixteenth century. Wyclif's *Opus Evangelicum* is his statement that the faith found in Scripture is sufficient for the regulation of the whole Church in the world.[31] The faith as set out in the Sermon on the Mount contains all that is needful to govern everyone in this life, without the addition of any 'human tradition'.[32] No other law has force unless it conforms to this. In the days of the first beginnings of the Church, that was understood, and indeed the apostles and their followers were 'ruled by the pure law of the Gospel'.[33] Hus too gives a definition of a heretic which takes Scripture to be the only secure test. 'A heretic, properly speaking and strictly is someone who insistently contradicts the word of Holy Scripture, in writing or in deed'. There are three essential elements in this definition. There must be an error in understanding, a falsehood which is contrary to Holy Scripture, persistence in the wrong opinion.[34] Dissent from the teaching of an institutional Church on which Hus no longer felt able to rely is no indicator of heresy; it therefore does not enter into this definition.

Areas Where Disagreement May be Allowed

In the present day, the question tends to be whether the Christian ought to be looking for a fixed point of reference at all. The twentieth century saw fundamental challenges from academic theologians, which continue into the twenty-first. Mid-twentieth-century 'Process' theology explored the idea that God is not the changeless being of the early Christian world but a dynamic force, himself able to alter. Other theologians have interpreted the death of Christ as a message to the world that God himself is vulnerable. Others still have spoken of the 'death of God' and the 'post-Christian world'.

Where missionaries in the nineteenth century had taken a ready-made faith and with it a good deal of the culture of the West and imposed them upon the communities of new Christians they won to the faith, twentieth-century missionaries became more sensitive to the cultures of others. There was talk of 'inculturation', the degree to which Christianity could and should accommodate itself to the culture it enters. In parts of Africa polygamy is the social norm. Should Christians in such societies be allowed to have more than one spouse?

There was some recognition even before the twentieth century that not every difference of opinion ought to be 'church-dividing'. Some things may not matter; they may be questions on which Christians remain free to take different views. A variety of different points have presented themselves in different periods as 'unresolved questions' on which the Church has taken no settled view and on which there is therefore no orthodoxy. Many of these have remained 'things indifferent' (*adiaphora*), and therefore matters on which no position (within a certain range of options) is 'heretical'. The origin of the soul is an important example. Both Augustine (354–430) and Anselm of Canterbury (1033–1109) left unsettled the question whether God makes a fresh soul for each child which is conceived (the 'creationist' theory) or the soul is somehow inherited or handed on with the body which is conceived (the '*traducianis*' theory). John Wyclif discusses whether the world was created *successive vel subita*, over a series of 'days' as it says in Genesis, or in a single divine act. He explains that Augustine and those who follow him seem to disagree with other sources who have taken a view on this matter. Possibly, he suggests, learned men who seem to hold the opposite opinion to Augustine's were speaking only *opinative* (as a matter of opinion).[35]

In practice the decision that something really matters has often been precipitated by those who hold dissident opinions, when they have pressed them insistently against the stated objections of the Church's 'authorities' until the matter has become an 'issue'. There comes a moment when there are formal condemnations and an area of 'orthodoxy' comes into being which was previously not crystallized. That is where 'the importance of unity' comes to the test.

This has been a chapter with a presumption – that unity is best for the Church and for believers, because it is what Christ intended. That certainty has been central to the ecumenical movement of the last century. For centuries before it was the justification both for trying to get agreement and for excluding those who would not agree, sometimes subjecting them to extremely harsh treatment, to compel them to 'conform'. In today's world 'diversity' and 'tolerance' have an attraction earlier centuries did not so easily recognize. So a running question as we move on will be whether this call for unity still stands up as securely as it did.

Chapter 2

The Boundaries of Orthodoxy: Faith

Vincent of Lérins (d. before 450) laid down a famous test of the true faith in his *Commonitorium*. He said the true faith is what is believed 'everywhere, always and by everyone' (*quod ubique, quod semper, quod ab omnibus creditum est*).

One of the most natural vehicles for the expression of the key points of the faith in a way the faithful can grasp, and know by heart, has been the 'creed' (from *credo*, 'I believe'). This had two early roles. One was baptismal. The Christian convert affirming his or her faith at the moment of baptism could conveniently say a short paragraph in the presence of the congregation, so as to join his or her faith with theirs. The other was liturgical in a more general way. In worship, particularly at the Lord's Supper or Eucharist, the congregation could affirm the faith of the community together in a single form of words, often in a formal 'dialogue' in which questions were asked and responses given.

The first such formulae were very simple. 'Jesus is Lord' appears in 1 Corinthians 12.3, Romans 10.9, Philippians 2.11.[1]

Other important points which were to emerge in the Creeds are already there in the New Testament. There is the statement that Jesus is the Son of God (Mark 3.11, Luke 4.3, Acts 9.20) and the recognition of the pivotal character of the resurrection (Romans 4.24, 10.9; I Thessalonians 1.10). There are elements of the doctrine of the Trinity in Matthew 28.19 and in 2 Corinthians 13.14. In 1 Corinthians 8.6, 15.3–5 and 1 Timothy 2.5 occur more elaborated accounts of the faith. These can be seen as the natural outgrowths of the process of winning converts, teaching new Christians the faith and bringing them into the community by baptism.

Bringing these and other key beliefs together in an orderly way eventually led to the emergence of solid all-embracing statements which could be relied on everywhere. The two most important examples are the text known as the 'Apostles' Creed' and the Nicene Creed.

The Apostles' Creed

It was important that any statement of the faith on which great reliance was to be placed should carry an authority as close to that of Christ himself and his Apostles as possible. A tradition grew up that the Apostles themselves had left a creed containing all that was needful. In its present form the 'Apostles' Creed' is first found in the eighth century, but it is certainly older, with versions in local use from at least the fourth century. It may go back to the first period of the Roman Church. No Council of the Church formally approved it; it gained its currency from use and acceptance, and its authority from the belief that it was the work of Jesus's own Apostles. It was used in the Middle Ages in the baptism service, and it is thus important as a statement of the beliefs of a candidate for baptism.

Plate 1 Communion of the Apostles, fresco by Fra Angelico (1387–1455). Museo di San Marco, Florence/photo SCALA.

It was known as the *symposium*, because of a story which was in circulation from about the end of the fourth century, that the Apostles sat together round a table to make it up, each contributing a clause. Rufinus, Jerome's rival, wrote an explanation of the origin of this creed early in the fifth century. He describes how, as the Apostles separated to go out into the world at the Lord's command, they 'agreed' the faith in a fixed form of words so that there should be no danger of divergence:

> As they were therefore on the point of taking leave of one another, they first settled an agreed norm of their future preaching, so that they might not find themselves, widely separated as they would be, giving out different doctrines. . . . So they met together in one spot and, being filled with the Holy Spirit, compiled this brief token . . . each making the contribution he thought fit; and they decreed that it should be handed out as standard teaching to all believers.[2]

This story, which is older than Rufinus, gave an authority to what had become known as the 'Apostles' Creed' which preserve its status alongside that of the Nicene Creed created by the Council of Nicaea in 325 at the height of the Arian crisis. Throughout the Middle Ages it was accepted that the Apostles' Creed was indeed the work of the Apostles. The important question is how far it is ultimately 'apostolic' in the wider sense of 'deriving from the earliest period of the Church'. It seems clear that it did emerge in that way, perhaps especially through its use in liturgy. The Apostle's Creed runs as follows:

> I believe in God the Father Almighty,
> Maker of heaven and earth:
> And in Jesus Christ his only Son our Lord,

Who was conceived by the Holy Ghost,
Born of the Virgin Mary,
Suffered under Pontius Pilate,
Was crucified, dead, and buried:
He descended into hell;
The third day he rose again from the dead;
He ascended into heaven,
And sitteth on the right hand of God the
Father Almighty;
From thence he shall come to judge the
quick and the dead.
I believe in the Holy Ghost;
the holy Catholic Church;
the Communion of Saints;
the forgiveness of sins;
the resurrection of the body;
and the life everlasting.

However, the task of setting out the faith in a short statement intended to be 'internalized' by each believer and each congregation as it became known and familiar, proved to be only the first step. In the New Testament, there are already hints of trouble to come. The first letter of John (4.2) and also his second letter (v.7) touch on the incipient question of what it can mean to speak of the human nature of Christ. John says that you may know a Christian by whether he or she acknowledges that Jesus Christ was truly man.

This was to become an immensely important question for the first Christian centuries. Ignatius (c.35–107)[3] placed a considerable emphasis on the belief that Christ was resurrected in his physical human body. That was necessary to counter the teaching of dualist Gnostics, determined to separate body and soul, matter and spirit, who said that the resurrected Christ was solely divine, and no longer had a real human body, or perhaps had never had one at all. The struggle for clarity on this point runs throughout the early centuries. For this was an age when the influence of Platonism remained strong among Christian intellectuals and apologists.

Platonists found it difficult to come to terms with any idea of God which did not put him so high as to be almost above Being itself. The nearest most Platonists could come to a 'Trinity' was to envisage a Supreme Being, with a 'Logos', or 'Word', or rational principle who was subordinate to the Supreme Being, and a World Soul subordinate to the Logos, which was able to engage directly with the material world by dwelling within it as part of that world. The Logos was naturally equated with Christ in such schemes of explanation. It was a huge step to believe the Logos to be truly man, with real flesh, able to suffer and die like other human beings. It was also an enormous step to believe in a Trinity of Persons equal and co-eternal and of the same substance, and not forming a hierarchy of divine or semi-divine beings.

These skirmishes with the philosophers on points central to the Christian faith led to the creation of an extensive early Christian literature of 'apologetic', or defence of the faith. The early apologists, or defenders of the faith, were often in difficulties because it was still not easy to point to a statement of what is constitutive for Christian belief, which went into sufficient detail to cover this kind of problem. Justin Martyr in the second century could criticize leaders of mistaken opinion for 'calling themselves Christians', but it was not possible for him to show beyond question what they ought to be saying if they really *were* Christians.[4]

The Nicene Creed

The Nicene Creed, which has provided a point of reference for most Christians ever since, was drafted for the Council of Nicaea in 325, in a period of active controversy, and amended by the Council of Constantinople in 381. Its main contents are really much older, and probably derive from the Baptismal Creed of ancient Christian Jerusalem, or something similar. In the late fifth century the custom seems to have begun of reciting it after the Gospel had been read in the Eucharist, or service of Holy Communion so, like the Apostles' Creed, it was regularly used in worship and became extremely familiar as a touchstone or benchmark of right belief.

> I believe in one God the Father Almighty,
> Maker of heaven and earth,
> And of all things visible and invisible;
> And in one Lord Jesus Christ, the only-begotten
> Son of God,
> Begotten of his Father before all worlds,
> God of God, light of light,
> Very God of very God,
> Begotten not made,
> Being of one substance with the Father,
> By whom all things were made;
> Who for us men and for our salvation came
>   down from heaven,
> And was incarnate by the Holy Ghost of
> the Virgin Mary,
> And was made man,
> And was crucified also for us under Pontius Pilate,
> He suffered and was buried, and the third day he
>   rose again according to the Scriptures,

And ascended into heaven,
And sitteth on the right hand of the Father.
And he shall come again with glory to judge both
the quick and the dead:
Whose Kingdom shall have no end.
And I believe in the Holy Ghost
The Lord and giver of life,
Who proceedeth from the Father and the Son,
Who with the Father and the Son together is
worshipped and glorified,
Who spake by the prophets.
And I believe in one catholic and apostolic Church.
I acknowledge one baptism for the remission of sins.
And I look for the resurrection of the dead, and
the life of the world to come.
Amen.

Several of its clauses are directed against those with
doubts over the true divinity and humanity of Christ, such
as the followers of the contemporary heretics Arius, who
were known as the 'Arians' (see chapter 4). So the main
reason for the framing of the Nicene Creed was the urgent
need to provide an official statement to settle the 'Arian
controversy'.

These clauses emphasize the divinity of Christ, the fact
that he is eternal, and that his substance is the same divine
substance as that of the Father.

And in one Lord Jesus Christ, the only-begotten
Son of God
Begotten of his Father before all
God of God, light of light
Very God of very God
Begotten not made

Being of one substance with the Father
By whom all things were made

The next group stress his humanity:

Who for us men and for our salvation came down from
   heaven,
And was incarnate by the Holy Ghost of the Virgin Mary,
And was made man.

Another area of contemporary preoccupation which is reflected in the clauses of the Nicene Creed was the 'dualist' solution to the problem of good and evil (see chapter 6). The 'dualists' (who were known as the Gnostics even before the lifetime of Jesus) and later as the Manichees, Cathars, Bogomils or Albigensians), held that there are two great powers in the universe, a good God and and evil God, equally strong and locked in eternal conflict for control of the cosmos. The dualists attributed the creation of matter (or visible things) to the evil God, and the creation of the invisible spirit or soul to the good God. They held that as a result there is a 'war' inside every human being between body and soul, with physical longings pulling one way and spiritual aspirations the other. The creed sums this up by emphasizing that the God of the Christians made both matter and spirit, visible and invisible worlds:

I believe in one God the Father Almighty
Maker of heaven and earth
And of all things visible and invisible

These clauses emphasize that there is only one God and that he is omnipotent, not merely one of a pair of opposed forces in the universe engaged in eternal warfare. The Creed insists that he is also the maker of the physical world.

Some heretics over the centuries questioned the resurrection, which was of central importance to the Christian faith. Everything turned on Jesus having truly risen from the dead. Only if Jesus was really the Son of God and really human and really died and was truly resurrected was the Christian faith not in vain, for Christ's resurrection is the guarantee of ours, the final warrant that he was indeed the Son of God. These points are insisted on in the Creed. It showed the power of God in Christ and gave assurance to the faithful that they were saved and could hope for heaven.

> And was crucified also for us under Pontius Pilate,
> He suffered and was buried, and the third day
>   he rose again according to the Scriptures,
> And ascended into heaven,
> And sitteth on the right hand of the Father.

Finally comes the affirmation of Christ's authority as judge:

> And he shall come again with glory to
>   judge both the quick and the dead:
> Whose Kingdom shall have no end.

Questions about the Holy Spirit in the first Christian generations turned on his divinity and his equality with the Father and the Son, rather than on his role as Comforter. The area of dispute here tended to be whether he was truly divine and not merely some sort of animating force in the world (the World Soul) as some Platonists had said. The fact that he was of the same divine 'substance' (consubstantiality) and with the Father and was co-eternal with him was as important to emphasize as it was for Christ, for the philosophers' 'hierarchy' was always hovering. It was the 'educated man's' preference.

> And I believe in the Holy Ghost,
> The Lord and giver of life,
> Who proceedeth from the Father and the Son,
> Who with the Father and the Son together
>   is worshipped and glorified,
> Who spake by the prophets.

Questions about the role and nature and authority of the Church became much more complex in the West in the Middle Ages than they had been in the Church at large, at the time of the Council of Nicaea in 325. At the time of the formulation of the Nicene Creed the main thing which needed to be stressed was the fact that the Church was 'one': that it was a single 'communion' or *koinonia*, a particular kind of community which could also be thought of as the 'body' whose 'head' is Christ; that it was 'universal' or 'catholic' (one Church throughout the world); that it was 'apostolic' (engaged in mission as Jesus said he meant it to be and in continuity with his teaching).

> I believe in one catholic and apostolic Church

Questions about sin and the forgiveness of sin and the role of the sacraments arose in new and much more complicated ways in the Middle Ages, but at the time of the formation of the creeds one key question was whether the Church had authority to declare God's forgiveness of sins. Another concerned the role of baptism in the remission of sins. It was also actively discussed whether baptism could be repeated. So the creed refers simply to these key points:

> I acknowledge one baptism for the remission of sins

Questions about the purpose and end of human life were also in their early stages of 'thinking through' when the creeds were completed. It is an indication of the continuing importance of the battle to outlaw dualism that it had to be stressed that not only the soul but the material body would be resurrected.

> And I look for the resurrection of the dead,
> and the life of the world to come.

The discussion of the creeds goes on in a modern ecumenical context. The creeds are shared by the vast majority of Christian churches even when they are formally divided from one another. The World Council of Churches' *Confessing the One Faith: An Ecumenical Explication of the Apostolic Faith*[5] is the fruit of a project designed to clarify these large areas of continuing common ground in the ancient creeds.

Catechesis

The focus on the creeds encouraged increasingly systematic teaching by way of catechesis, or instruction, of the adults who were converted to the faith. It is not possible to become a heretic by accident. Heresy involves choice, and perseverance in an opinion when the Church has pronounced it wrong. It has not been regarded as heresy to discuss whether something might be a heresy, or to raise a question about a point of faith, especially when the purpose was to establish where the right view lay and to set out a 'confession of faith' or statement of belief. The question was whether to introduce into the teaching of catechumens (converts under instruction in preparation for baptism) an element of real discussion, so that they could get such uncertainties resolved or 'out of their systems'.

Augustine found that unavoidable. Teaching new converts the key points of their faith in keeping with the profession of faith they would make when they were baptized did not prevent their being aware as educated articulate adults that they had unanswered questions. Augustine's *De Catechizandis Rudibus* ('on catechizing the simple') was written in response to an enquiry from a deacon of Carthage who was conscious that he was not clear what essentials he should be teaching or how best to convey them. Augustine's response reflects his own testing experiences with adult converts, who in late Roman society might be anything but 'simple'. In north Africa particularly, as the educated, articulate and angry pagans arrived there in exile from Italy, a catechist might well find himself 'defending' the faith rather than merely 'teaching' it. There were questions the converts wanted answered about the reasons why the Christian God had allowed a Christian Empire to fall to barbarian invaders, and they had to leave their homes and flee.

Augustine describes a process in which there is naturally a good deal of persuasion, for persuasiveness was his stock-in-trade as an orator. He explains how to pick up any perception expressed by the catechumen which is along the right lines, and develop it so that the would-be new Christian is brought to see the beauty and rightness of Christian truth. He encourages the Christian teacher to point

Plate 2　St Augustine teaching in Rome, fresco by Benozzo Gozzoli, 1464–5. Sant'Agostino, San Gimignano/photo SCALA.

to stages in the story and then let it unfold, so that it is as though the convert saw Jacob following his twin out of the womb with his hand round his ankle (Genesis 25.26). It is to be expected that those who have some knowledge of the arguments against the truth of the Christian faith and the reasons why others are Jews or pagans will present those arguments and reasons and ask to be satisfied. They are likely to enquire why, if there is only one God and he is omnipotent, he allows these other schools of thought to arise and to persist. Augustine's answer is that God foresaw all this and that he intends that Christians should be tested in their faith.

The Augustinian expectations apply in the case of adult converts in a world where a level of sophistication is to be expected in the philosophical knowledge of educated adults, in a way which is not possible where the teaching of the faith chiefly involves children. Nevertheless, believers' baptism had not precluded the baptizing of infants, and it had not been in doubt that baptism was a sacrament in which divine grace was at work. In Augustine's own lifetime, there was a shift in the West from adult to infant baptism. The doctrines that an individual could be baptized only once, coupled with the confidence that baptism took away both the guilt and the penalty for original sin and also for any actual sins someone had committed, had encouraged even committed Christians to put off the moment of baptism as long as possible, so as to give themselves less time to sin again. But that argument worked powerfully, too, in the case of infants, for infant morality was high and Augustine was not the only bishop to hold that an unbaptized infant could not enter the presence of God and spend eternity in heaven.

Ironically, one of the heretical movements against which Augustine actively wrote and preached sharpened this question. The Pelagians took it that all that was needed was a resolute following of Christ; a human being need not sin if he or she tried hard, and there was no inheritance of sinfulness (original sin) from Adam to be taken into account. Augustine's response to that had the effect of strengthening still further the doctrine of baptism, and it was not without its effect on the Pelagians themselves. A number of them came to Augustine quietly to have their children baptized just in case he was right.

From the move to infant baptism came in due course another style of catechesis, designed to form young minds, rather than discuss issues in the way that was necessary with older ones. These took the form of questions and standard answers, which the child simply learned by heart.

Misdirected Worship and Taking the Name of God in Vain

A good deal of the teaching which has caused most anxiety because it disturbed the unity of the faith has done so because it was so close to the accepted truth and yet not quite 'there'. It has often derived from a desire to protect something precious. Dualism, the belief that there are two opposing supreme powers in the universe, for example, can be fired by a wish to preserve the goodness of God from the faintest imputation of responsibility for evil. Resistance to a corrupt power structure in the Church can be inspired by an indignant sense that this was not the way Jesus said he wanted his disciples to behave. But there are also examples of something closer to 'impiety' in different forms: either wholly misplaced and misdirected worship, such as idolatry, or sheer apathy. There are biblical passages disapproving of idolatry. Moses had three thousand

Israelites put to death to punish them for worshipping the golden calf instead of the one true God (Exodus 32.25–9). The blasphemer who breaks the commandment not to take the name of God lightly (Exodus 20.7) can even be stoned to death for cursing the name of God (Leviticus 24.10–14).

Idolatry is forbidden in Exodus. It is one of the ten commandments that God only is to be worshipped and not idols (Exodus 20.3–5). Yet idolatry has been a temptation for various reasons in the history of Christianity. Paul praises the Christians in Thessalonia because they have turned from idols to serve the living God (1 Thessalonians 1.9). The decision to give up idolatry in the early Christian centuries was a decision to withdraw from the normal expectations of pagan society. It involved a commitment to a religion which was not willing to participate in the general syncretism which allowed pagans to equate Zeus with Jupiter and so on, without any sense of disloyalty to their gods. Ordinary Christians found this a difficult rule to keep to. It is evident that the cult of the saints tended only too easily to replace in the popular mind the old worship of small local deities.

This did not provoke a real crisis for some centuries. In the Iconoclast Controversy of the Greek East in the eighth and ninth centuries, the question was how far the veneration of holy pictures was compatible with the worship of a God who could not be contained in (nor could he be represented by) any image. The enthusiasm for icons had latterly reached a point where it seemed to some to amount to idolatry, while to others it was merely an appropriate expression of religious awe and veneration for the sacred. There was a social aspect, too. The power of the monks was a serious concern to the imperial authorities.

Part of the trouble has been the sophistication with which the various 'uses' of images need to be distinguished if the worshipper is to stay clear of the 'worship of idols' when he or she 'venerates' a holy picture or the relic of a saint. The great fear of the Church's authorities has been the contamination of the purity of focus of the faith of the Christian. Many reformers were also concerned that making and paying for statues used money and wealth which could have been employed in helping the poor. Even sixteenth-century conservatives and moderates were uncomfortable with anything which looked like a tendency towards idolatry. Thomas More kept images out of his Utopia. Erasmus was unenthusiastic about them.

At one extreme the use of images may seem best avoided altogether, since no image can do justice to the transcendency of God. That was the position generally taken by the sixteenth-century reformers and their heirs. It informed Puritanism and led to the stripping bare of the churches of many Protestant communities in which nothing was to be seen except perhaps a text from the Bible on the wall or a plain cross. It could also work up extremists to carry out works of destruction, as happened when the annual religious procession was cancelled at Ghent in 1566 because of 'portents' (an altar of the Virgin had burned down) and people ran amok, egging each other on to break down images and crosses and to ransack churches. Less than a century later, Oliver Cromwell's followers ransacked the mediaeval churches of England, destroying stained glass and pictures and statues. A more moderate view refrains from worship or even veneration of images of God and holy things but recognizes that signs and symbols can be helpful as teaching aids.

Others take a position which begins to cross a line towards 'worship' of images. They recognize that images may be numinous, and they try to draw power from them to help them with difficulties in their lives. Throughout the Middle Ages, the relics of a saint were considered to have within them a store of the saint's unused merits. The faithful could pray to the saint to have such powers 'applied' for their own benefit or that of those they loved. It was noticed in the Church of South India in the twentieth century that Hindus who were converted to Christianity were sometimes shocked by the Christian use of images, but that they were often able to feel at home with this kind of thing. The extreme and ultimately 'pagan' position is that the image itself is the deity.

Another face of the danger of losing the wholehearted 'focus' on God which Christianity demands is the casualness or offensiveness towards the deity which amounts to blasphemy, the 'treason against God'. This idea was important in the early Church, with its high respect for the deity. The Code of the Emperor Justinian (529–65) says that God is so angry if blasphemy is not punished that famine, earthquake and pestilence are likely to follow. At the end of the Middle Ages, Calvin and Luther returned to the idea of blasphemy, and helped to make it important again. Calvin was instrumental in procuring the execution of Michael Servetus (1511–53), who had been repudiating the doctrine of the Trinity. A friend of Calvin's denounced him to the Inquisition. He was imprisoned, but escaped. Calvin had him rearrested and burnt as a heretic when he refused to recant.

Does the Faith 'Develop' Through History?

Vincent of Lérins's 'dictum' that the true faith is what is believed always, everywhere and by everyone, assumes that 'the faith', once decided and stated, can remain a settled thing 'always'. Yet even if it is maintained that for there to be continuity over time, the faith must be the same, it manifestly cannot be held in identical words in every place and in every century. It is in that change of language and shift of cultural context that the question of 'development of doctrine' arises.

In the middle of the nineteenth century, John Henry Newman was writing about the implications of the 'development' or restating of doctrine age by age, at exactly the time when he himself was led by Vincent of Lérins's dictum to move from the Church of England to the Roman Catholic Church. He had come to the conclusion that the belief 'held always, everywhere and by everyone' was to be met with only in the Roman Catholic communion, and that was therefore the safest place to be. He wrote a letter to the Marquise de Salvo (15 December 1845) in which he said, 'I seriously think it unsafe for anyone to remain out of the Catholic Church who is aware of the fact that he is without it'.[6] In a letter of 8 November 1845 he was explaining that 'it would have been gross hypocrisy in me, to profess to rule myself by the early Church, and yet to remain in a communion which resembled the Donatists, or Nestorians, or Monophysites, and not the ancient Catholic Church'.[7] These were ideas which could also have been met with in William Chillingworth in the seventeenth century. 'I thought,' he says, 'that there was and must be always in the world some church that could not err',[8] but although that made him become a Roman Catholic for a time it did not prevent him returning in the end to the Church of England.

In the same autumn as Newman was expressing these concerns and becoming a Roman Catholic, he was correcting

Plate 3 John Henry Newman, portrait bust by Thomas
Woolner, 1867. By permission of the Warden and Fellows of
Keble College, Oxford.

the proof-sheets of his *Essay on the Development of Doctrine*. In the opening pages, he urges a different, though not incompatible principle: 'A development will have this characteristic, that, its action being in the busy scene of human life, it cannot progress at all without cutting across, and thereby destroying or modifying or incorporating within itself existing modes of thinking and operating'. There will, in other words, be subtle and complex changes as the faith is stated afresh for each generation. Newman did not think that 'the stream is clearer near the spring'; on the contrary, he thought this does not apply to belief which, on the contrary is 'more equable, and purer, and stronger, when its bed has become deep, and broad, and full'.[9] Here his thinking was in tune with the assumptions of many in the eighteenth century, that there had been progress in theology since the earliest days. It is in striking contrast with the desire to return to the apostolic ways,which we shall meet in chapter 5.

Bible or Church? Is there a fixed point of reference? In the end, Newman opted for the Church, in which he found the most convincing continuity of faith and teaching with the early Church. Others, especially among the Protestant communities which had survived the Reformation, turned to the Bible. The dilemma is expressed in an entertaining note by Isaak Walton (1593–1683) of an exchange between Sir Henry Wotton and a Roman Catholic priest. 'Where was your religion to be found before Luther?' asked the priest. 'My religion was to be found then, where yours is not to be found now, in the written Word of God,' answered Sir Henry.[10] Attitudes of this kind show how far things had moved from the early recognition that it is artificial to separate Bible and Church.

So the emergence of 'creeds' as convenient and reliable brief statements of faith has a history both in their use in worship, when the community affirmed its faith collectively, and in the instruction of the faithful. It also has a place in the defence of the faith against heresy. Alongside the idea of faith as a state or condition of the soul, an affective disposition towards God and a commitment to him, stands the question what exactly it *was* that Christians believed, what was the *content* of this belief. We shall see as we go on how that was challenged.

There is one further consequence of the steady imposition of a requirement to bow to the teaching authority of the Church, where there is a heavy emphasis on conformity of faith under an increasingly monarchical authority. This is to be seen in the papacy in the late Middle Ages when it prompted the revolution which is now known as the Reformation. It has had a recurrence from time to time in the later history of the papacy. In recent generations the Swiss Roman Catholic theologian Hans Küng was only one of the theologians deprived of his licence to teach because he was asking questions which were not permitted by the Vatican. This kind of repressive determination to force compliance is not confined to the universal primacy. It has been a very common feature of small sects, too. It is by no means easy to strike and maintain a balance between freedom of enquiry and openness to fresh insights 'within' the faith and tyranny over freedom of speech and worship, and even of thought. For the disciplining of heretics is in the end the act of a 'thought police'. But a liberal approach to 'heresy' sets the continuity of the faith at risk. The dilemma is real.

The reason for separating the questioning which has led to the fuller formulation of statements of the 'true faith' from the problem of the challenge to order, which forms the subject of the next chapter, is that the Church itself has always seen a significant difference. Differences about order need not be Church-dividing, though they often have been. But there has always been a strong confidence, until the twentieth century, that there could be only one faith.

Chapter 3

The Boundaries of Orthodoxy: Order

When Christians met in a Council, the Holy Spirit was expected to influence a prayerful 'forming of the common mind'. It was also recognized that the Holy Spirit might be saying something to the Church through an individual. Nevertheless, individuals who believe themselves to be personally led by the Holy Spirit have been a source of concern to the organized Church from the beginning when they question whether it is God's will that they should be confined within the formal bounds of the community or required to conform to its rules. There was, in other words, a potential tension between the 'charism', or special gift of grace to an individual, and 'order', the regular way of doing things, in which the Church was seen to act as a community.

'Disorder' at the Wild Fringes

This challenging character of those who claim to be Spirit-led as individuals has been particularly notable in the fiery, in whose eyes has shone the light of prophecy. They did not die away with the first generations. They reappear in various guises, such as that of the 'pentecostal' proselytizing zealots of later ages. (The modern Pentecostal churches have a place in this tradition, but they are merely one of its developments.)

Some of the 'Spirit-led' have also 'rejected the world' in a dramatic manner. The concept of the 'world-renouncer' is not confined to Christian history. It is found in Buddhism, too, for example.[1] Christianity had some success in 'containing' the desire to become 'an outsider for God' within the formal structures of the religious 'orders'. A community life was the norm for religious in the West, at least from the time of Benedict of Nursia (c.480–550), who founded a monastery at Monte Cassino from which sprang Benedictine monasticism. Hermits were the exception and they frequently had a link with a nearby monastery, living the eremitical (hermit) life in its grounds. In the East, where idiosyncratic and idiorhythmic patterns of religious life were more usual, they were still to some degree 'contained' by the strictness of the expectation that there would be respect for a profoundly ascetic discipline.

The extremists, the radical world-renouncers subjugating the flesh to dramatic excess, might be perceived as a threat even where they were living lives of seclusion. But in some places the radicals and extremists were far from invisible. The geographical coincidences are not in themselves significant but they help to set the picture in context. There were flagellants in the fourteenth and fifiteenth century in the region of Erfurt and Mühlhausen in Germany, where other forms of heretical belief had previously flourished and where some of the most radical of the sixteenth century reformers were later to be found. The immediate prompter of the popularity of the movement was probably the fear created by the epidemic of plague. It is hard to classify the beliefs of these groups tidily or even confidently. These flagellants condemned the official Church as the Church of Antichrist. They described sacraments as human inventions without scriptural foundation. On that basis they rejected marriage. They relied on 'be fruitful and multiply' (Genesis 1.22) as a justification for promiscuous sexual intercourse. They held the reborn to be sinless, and therefore unable to act wrongly. They rejected the veneration of saints, the swearing of oaths, the very use of church buildings. They practised baptism by blood. Some heretics of this type came to be called 'Bloodfriends'.

The Brethren of the Free Spirit are found as early as the twelfth century in what is now Switzerland and the Rhineland area of Germany. In 1212 several adherents of this sect were burned alive outside the city walls of Strasbourg. In the wake of the heretical and dissident movements in the later Middle Ages they and their like flourished across the territories where German and Dutch were spoken. They had some tenets in common, particularly the use of the vernacular for religious writings, and rejection of the sacraments, although the Brethren tended to have a particularly mystical bent.[2]

One of the results of the heightening of talk of heresy was that those groups which came under suspicion might be labelled almost at random, and gossip flourished, so that rumours of secret meetings, devil worship, magical practices, sexual misbehaviour and assorted forms of Satanism ran about, linked to various individuals and groups.[3] By the fourteenth century it was whispered that the Adamites held rites in the nude and the Luciferans worshipped the Devil, both sects with links with the Brethren of the Free Spirit. These rumours are themselves evidence of the tensions created by the appearance of charismatic phenomena and anything which hinted at a disregard for the order imposed by the Church.

But at the other end of the spectrum such figures seemed to some commentators pillars of rectitude and examples to the faithful. Lay movements seeking to return to the apostolic life, such as the Beghards (male) and Beguines (female), sometimes fell into this category. Believers of quite different habits, sober, hard-working at plain manual labour, vowed to chastity, were also frequently linked by repute with the Brethren of the Free Spirit and their like. Whatever their real merits or demerits, the wild figures on the fringe and the more sober would-be reformers both created a sense of unease in the authorities because they did not fit into the orderly structure of the Church.

If little reliance can be placed on descriptions of extraordinary activities and excesses as a basis for the classification of the early mediaeval movements, much the same problem of a polarization of the 'exemplary' and the 'mad' presents itself in succeeding centuries. The Anabaptists include a number of groups in sixteenth century Europe who refused to baptize infants and said that baptism should be a commitment made by adults who could affirm their faith for themselves (believers' baptism); in some cases they refrained from baptism altogether. Menno Simons, founder of the Mennonites, argued that baptism is not a sacrament, in the sense of a mystery which transforms the individual baptized and frees him or her of sin, but merely a ceremony signifying something which is already the case. We are not reborn as a result of being baptized, he explains; we are reborn by faith and by the Word of God.

As in the case of the mediaeval Free Spirit groups, such ideas were associated with others, sometimes tending to extremes on the fringes of orthodoxy and orthopraxis; sometimes merging into what were partly political uprisings; sometimes simply holding to the simplicity of life that Christ urged on his followers, and making the preservation of peace central. This pacificism was characterized by passive resistance and the refusal to take oaths which runs as a common threat through so much dissidence in the Middle Ages. The Anabaptist sects associated the resistance to oath-taking with the confidence that sacraments, like the laws of the Church, were unnecessary to those who had faith. Antinomianism – the idea that Christian faith sets the believer free from any obligation to obey a law, moral or civil – is a different idea, but capable of attracting a group of adherents.

The faces of Anabaptism were numerous. Thomas Müntzer (c.1490–1525) appears in place after place preaching Anabaptist ideas. The Zwickau Prophets in Wittenberg in the 1520s held a doctrine of the Inner Light much like that of George Fox a century later. This relied on an inward conviction or experience as the most reliable source of knowledge about salvation. These Prophets were sufficiently revolutionary in the political sense to associate themselves with the uprising of the German peasants in 1525. Others stressed the common ownership of property. In Münster there appeared in the 1530s a group of Anabaptists who believed they could establish a Kingdom of Saints, and tried to seize the city so that they could turn it into the New Jerusalem. They began to practise polygamy, and other extreme and fanatical habits seem to have appeared among them. The Swiss Brethren practised believers' baptism; like the Mennonites, who stressed pacificism, in the aftermath of the happenings at Münster. Melchiorites or Münsterites were communities of Anabaptists who followed the teaching of Melchior Hoffman, who seems to have held, like the early heretics who have been labelled Docetists, that Christ's humanity was a mere 'face' or 'dress', and his suffering a mere appearance. Their violent views (Müntzer held that the godless lost the right to live) gave Anabaptists a bad name.

Anabaptists were disliked – for their real or perceived views – by both the Roman Catholic Church and the more conventional reforming movements. Luther, Calvin and Zwingli all condemned them, mainly for their rejection of the sacraments, but partly, too, because they were setting themselves outside the reformed Church order as well as that of the Church the reformers were seeking to change. They suffered a good deal of persecution as a consequence.

George Fox (1624–91), the founder of the Society of Friends or Quakers, was outspoken in much the same way, and on many of the same points, when he preached reliance on the inner Word of God, the living Christ speaking in each soul. He was condemned for blasphemy and imprisoned. Yet in this case, the charismatic way was certainly not ultimately disruptive. In time the Quakers became a force for peace and set an example of simplicity of life. Aspects of the mainstream 'puritan' movement of the seventeenth century overlapped with this kind of moderate radical thinking; for dissent formed a continuum, one set of presumptions merging into another. Radical social programmes appear in other contexts, and the degree to which such groups as the Quakers formed pressure-groups for radical social change became apparent.

The Wesleys, the late eighteenth century founders of Methodism, placed a strong emphasis on the Holy Spirit, and on holiness. The 'Holiness' movement in the USA in the twentieth century began among the American Methodists in the second half of the nineteenth century, with no apparent intention at first of establishing separate demoninations. But their missionary activities soon led to that happening. The Pentecostal movement was a further development of all this charismatic tendency, beginning between about 1901 and 1906. The emphasis was on baptism with the Holy Spirit, which was said to bring a 'second blessing' of Christian perfection. Adherents prayed for a new Pentecost. The largely black congregations experienced ecstasy, trances, involuntary jerking, and they spoke in tongues. Here, as in earlier examples, there is potential for good and bad, often depending on the particular local leadership, for there can be no common order and no overall oversight.

A modern manifestation of the group which sets itself apart from the mainstream Church order, or at least exists only on its fringes, is the kind of 'sect' which attracts young people into a 'closed' community, separates them from their families and friends and sends them out into the streets to proselytize others for the community.

Orderliness

These examples of Christian practices, reaching a long way out into the extremes of what could be contained within a conventional ecclesiastical order, already make it plain that 'order' has had a rich variety of senses in the history of the Church's attitudes to heresy and schism. It is set within a profound confidence that God is in ultimate providential control of a universe where heresy is a symptom of Satan's determination to overthrow that control. It has been in the face of the challenge presented by this kind of thing that there has been such an insistence on 'order' in the Church.

In the Carolingian period, Florus of Lyons wrote a long poem, a 'Lament on Empire', in which heresy is portrayed as no longer firmly trodden under foot. It is getting out of hand. The bonds of peace are broken. As a result heresy is rising up and threatening order.[4] Anselm of Canterbury was later to speak of the *rectus ordo*, in which he includes notions of hierarchy and harmony. His main idea is that God is in charge of a universe which reflects in its essence the orderliness of the divine mind. This gives a cosmic context to order in the Church which came naturally to the medieval mind.

In the very late twelfth century, Joachim, abbot of Fiore (c.1132–1202), made prophecies about the coming of the end of the world. He described the period of the Old Testament as the Age of the Father and the period of the New Testament as the Age of the Son. The Age of the Spirit was the present time, leading to the end of the world. These three periods or *status* reflect the Trinitarian character of all creation. In the last age, Joachim believed, new orders of 'spiritual men' would arise, who would transform the Church and make it spiritual once more. There was enough potential danger to ecclesiastical order in these ideas to get him condemned by the Fourth Lateran Council in 1215 for remarks he had made on the Trinity. Among his ideas was the suggestion that the papacy of his time had been taken over by Antichrist. This theme of the Pope as Antichrist later became popular in the circles of 'anti-Establishment' dissidence, such as the Lollards. Wyclif discusses the date when Satan was released to take over the Church as Antichrist.[5] The idea also had currency in the sixteenth century, giving, as it did, a strong backing to anti-Papalist movements.

One of the repeating themes in allegations of heresy has been the fear, not of 'unworthy', but of 'unauthorized' ministers. In this sense, 'order' involved the evolution of a system for choosing the leaders of the community. It was important to be sure who had authority to preach the Gospel and minister the sacraments so as ensure that it was done both validly (so that they are properly performed) and efficaciously (so that they were effective). What roles the leaders of the community should fulfil and what kind of authority they should have, and where that authority should come from, was (and still is) the subject of debate. It is still the point of disagreement where ecumenical dialogue and rapprochement most commonly break down.

The vocabulary used for ministry in the New Testament is varied, and words like 'bishop' and 'presbyter' are clearly not being used there consistently or even in any technical sense recognizable in later centuries. Presbyters were 'elders' at first, rather than 'priests' (*sacerdotes*). Their leadership rather than their sacramental function was to the fore. The 'deacons' have a more clearly defined role in the early structure. They looked after the widows and orphans and distributed alms, occupying a humbler position than the bishops and presbyters or elders. But because they held the purse-strings they gained influence. By the time of the Council of Nicaea in 325 it was already necessary to put some curb on their powers.

Over the first centuries a 'ladder' was created or emerged, up which the candidate for the ministry climbed, from the diaconate to the priesthood and in some cases to the episcopate. The sacramental 'powers' of consecrating the bread and wine at the Eucharist and declaring absolution or forgiveness of sins, came to be reserved to priests. Only bishops could ordain priests and deacons. So powers to create and maintain the ministry settled into a fixed pattern, and with them assumptions about the role of those in the various main 'orders'.

Central to this system throughout the centuries leading up to the Reformation in the West was the episcopate. *Episcopos* means 'overseer' and the episcopal ministry became the ministry of oversight, and also the ministry of unity. Bishops had a responsibility for preaching the Word, and for maintaining faith and order in their dioceses. They represented their 'flocks' at the meetings of synods and councils in which the local or universal Church met from time to time to discuss matters of discipline and faith. This was perhaps their most important function in relation to the preservation of the unity of the Church, for those 'unanimous' gatherings were the occasions for the affirmation and expression of that unity.

The most important principle to emerge was that the Holy Spirit is the ultimate source of ministerial authority in the Church, but that this 'charism' has to be matched by an act or course of action within the Church's order. That has not been a recipe for consistency but for division and disorder. The idea is that God 'calls' to ministry by giving an individual an inward 'vocation' but also 'calls' by mechanisms within the Church, so that not everyone who 'feels called' is automatically made a minister by the mere 'feeling'. In addition, there is some form of commissioning. Episcopal churches have insisted that there must be laying on of hands in a visible succession from the time of the Apostles, and that any break in that line invalidates the call to ministry. The Donatists of north Africa in Augustine's time took that view. It became a key issue again in the sixteenth century. An area of debate in such churches is whether the Holy Spirit could choose 'directly', setting an individual apart for a 'charismatic' ministry as he wishes. All that is necessary is for the local worshipping community to accept their minister (the 'Congregationalist' way). But a small local community which feels free to act independently can easily fall into aberrant patterns of life, or – perhaps more importantly – give the impression to an anxious wider Church of doing so.

The Rigorist Dispute

One of the first serious challenges to unity came from the need to come to some agreement about what was to be done about the 'lapsed'. Cyprian, Bishop of Carthage (d. 258) and Novatian, a Roman priest, entered into a correspondence in which may be traced the painfulness of the dilemma which was created when Christians gave way under persecution and turned their back on their faith. Apostasy had always been taken seriously because of Jesus's saying that he who puts his hand to the plough and then looks back is not fit for the Kingdom of God (Luke 9.62). But in the climate of fear of the periods of persecution in the Roman Empire which took place at intervals before the end of the fourth century, it was understandable that some should falter for their own protection, out of fear of death. When the persecution ended some of them wished to come back. Was the Church to receive them? At first Novatian thought, like Cyprian, that the rule of lifetime excommunication and exclusion from the Church for anyone who apostatized should be relaxed in some cases. But he came to take the opposite extreme rigorist view, and on that basis was made a rival pope by the rigorist party. In the correspondence between Novatian and Cyprian about this time (c.250–1) we find Novatian writing to Cyprian 'What is either more appropriate in time of peace or more necessary during the warfare of persecution than to hold fast the due severity of divine rigour?'.[6] But letters against Novatian survive, one accusing him of a 'new cruelty' in destroying the hope of salvation and denying the mercy of the Father and despising the penitence of a Christian brother.[7]

Cyprian's milder approach was to sympathize with 'our brothers' who have been overthrown by persecution; he feels their wounds as his own. His concern is rather with the practice of resorting to such unofficial confessors as the martyrs (those who had been tortured for their faith), instead of going to the bishop for absolution. Even penitents whose sin is minor, Cyprian reminds his readers, have to have the imposition of hands by their bishop before they can be restored to the community. How much more important is that where the sin is great?[8] Cyprian is anxious to preserve Church order, just like the rigorists, but his emphasis is on Church discipline, on moral purity and almsgiving, and respect for chastity and he did not find that incompatible with generosity to the repentant sinner, even to the apostate who sincerely repents. Cyprian's *On the Lapsed* and *On Rebaptism* thus address key issues of the day for those who were prepared to allow the restoration of those who had abandoned their faith, either under persecution or by joining some heretical community.

It was, in Cyprian's view, of immense importance that it be clear that there could be no question of rebaptism. A Christian could be baptized only once. The restoration of penitents was something quite different. Cyprian differed from Augustine, however, in his attitude to the baptism of heretics. He rejected heretical baptism. Augustine by contrast thought that for those who had been baptized with water and in the name of the Trinity, even among heretics, there had been a true baptism and there could be no second baptism.

Schismatics

Cyprian's overriding concern was still to maintain unity, just as it had been for the first Christians and their leaders. He speaks of the 'mystery of unity' (*hoc unitatis sacramentum*) and of the 'bond of concord (*hoc vinculum concordiae*).[9] He associates this unity with the chastity and modesty and purity of the Church as the Bride of Christ.[10]

In his *On the Lapsed* (*De lapsis*), Cyprian expresses concern over the practice of the faithful of resorting to the 'martyrs' who had suffered torture, and who many of them believed to be consequently qualified to grant dispensation from penance and readmission to communion to the lapsed. Yet it is his conviction that there can be no official decision on this practice until the present persecution is over and the bishops can meet to decide what to do about it. It must be for the Church (acting as one) to settle the matter.

The Donatists became the most notable schismatic group of the early Christian centuries, partly because Augustine of Hippo wrote so much about them. Their division from the Catholic Church had come about because they would not accept Caecilian as Bishop of Carthage in 311. Their objection was that he had been consecrated by someone who had been a *traditor* during the persecution of Christians under the Emperor Diocletian. The *traditores* were those who 'handed over' the Scriptures to the authorities to save their skins. The position of Donatus and his followers was that these apostates could not thereafter exercise priestly or episcopal functions, even if they repented and were absolved. They accepted a freshly consecrated bishop instead and thus began a distinct line of ministerial succession, or, in their own view, continued the 'true' line. They did not differ in points of faith from the Catholics, merely in this all-important question of the purity and continuity of order, which prevented them worshipping with the Catholics or accepting the sacraments administered by their ministers.

The first theologian to attack their position was the north African bishop Optatus of Milevis (fl.c.370), in his treatise against Parmenianus the Donatist. He wanted forgiveness for the Donatists, who claimed that they alone had the true ministerial succession from the time of the Apostles; he did not wish to see the sons punished for the sins of their fathers, but he wanted them back in the fold. He speaks of the 'one faith'.[11] If the 'peace' which was Christ's gift to the Church remained 'whole and inviolate' and was not disturbed by the authors of schism, 'there would be no dissension today between us and our brothers'.[12]

However, as a result of the schism, there is no arguing with the Donatists. 'Mixed community' though the Church is, containing both those who are to be saved and those who are not, saints and sinners, it cannot hold together those who set themselves apart from the Church. The Holy Spirit's gifts to the Church can be present when it contains sinners but they cannot be present where there is heresy or schism.[13] Augustine takes the same broad line, in his own response to Parmenianus. He too emphasizes the importance of preserving 'the unity of the Spirit in the bond of peace' (Ephesians 4.3). It is his view, too, that the right way to behave is not to eject the schismatics themselves from the community but to drive out the evil of their views and persuade them to return to the fold.[14]

This approach became less easy to maintain when the divisions involved larger portions of the Christian community. When, for example, the schism of East and West took place in 1054 it produced two 'halves' of the Church, both of which regarded the other as having gone seriously astray. This was the first large-scale example of what became in the sixteenth century a whole new pattern of 'order' in the Church, in which continuing but separated ecclesial communities refused to recognize one another as Churches, while each claiming to be the true Church.

Diaspora

In the first century, Ignatius of Antioch disapproved of 'separate assemblies', which he defined as those which stand in opposition to their local bishop.[15] He was recognizing a problem already apparent in the Epistles of St Paul, that the local Church can itself be a natural place for schisms to arise. The same difficulty was still there when Jan Hus wrote to the people of Louny (after March 1411) to warn them against allowing themselves to give rise to schisms, which he couples with 'treacheries, envies, angers etc.' Hus seems to have in mind chiefly the kinds of internal disagreements which arise in a local community. 'If anyone among you is intractable and disseminates discords, admonish him as a brother among yourselves.'[16] Yet when it came to the great issues of the day, Hus came to believe that 'the schism among the people' was not to be helped, for Paul had prophesied that 'the son of iniquity shall not be revealed until the schism comes first' (2 Thessalonians 2.3, much adapted).[17]

A modern outflow of the complex of difficulties created by schism has been the determined adherence to their old 'local' ways of Churches in diaspora. This depends on the persistence of language and culture as much as on religious distinctiveness, but it can be a powerful preservative of familiar ways. The immigrants who came with a religion often kept to it, worshipping separately in a new country and in some cases not recognizing one another's Churches. When members of the Church of England first found themselves in America, the Bishop of London appointed a Commissary to serve as his representative. The first Commissary, James Blair (1656–1743) was appointed for Virginia, and under his superintendence churchgoers recreated for themselves a physical resemblance to the churches of home, with parsonages and glebe lands. In Maryland religious liberty was allowed and Anglican and Roman Catholic parishes were set up side by side. The Maryland commissary Thomas Bray founded the Society for Promoting Christian Knowledge (SPCK) in 1699 and the Society for the Propagation of the Gospel in Foreign Parts (SPG) in 1701. Faithfulness to the 'divisions' in which they arrived has been particularly noticeable among immigrants from Orthodox churches, who have kept apart in Greek Orthodox, Russian Orthodox, Ukranian Orthodox, Bulgarian Orthodox or Finnish Orthodox groups.

Orthopraxis

One of the ways in which the Greek East followed a different track from the Latin West, after the fall of the Roman

Empire, was in its growing emphasis on an 'orthodoxy of life' which is sometimes termed 'orthopraxis'. This meant, in essence, that the living of a good Christian life, especially a monastic life, and especially a spiritual monastic life, became as important as orthodoxy of faith.

Maximus the Confessor (c.580–662) was a leader of a movement which was in the end condemned as a heresy. This was the belief (known as Monothelitism) that the incarnate Christ had a single will and not both a divine and a human will.[18] For political reasons it had had some currency in the seventh century. So Maximus was not unaware of the importance of orthodoxy and he knew how easy it was to fall away from it. Nevertheless, he was strongly drawn to the mystical tradition represented by the works of the writer known as Pseudo-Dionyius (fl. c.500) and through that, to the position that the way to know God was through worship and prayer rather than through trying to frame beliefs as clearly as possible in words. The objective was the 'deification' of the faithful soul, as it grew more and more to resemble the divine in whose image and likeness it was made.

Gregory Palamas (c.1296–1359) wrote on this theme in his *Triads*, in the midst of the Hesychast controversy. The Hesychasts were monks who saw theology as a contemplative activity, a form of prayer, a discourse with God rather than an exercise in reasoning. The 'orthodox' monk living in this expectation strives to arrive at a permanent state of mental prayer, usually focusing on the name of Jesus and using the 'Jesus Prayer' in the spirit of Psalm 34.8, with its exhortation to 'taste and see that the Lord is good'. 'Have no other occupation or meditation,' said Nicephorus of Mount Athos in the fourteenth century, 'than the cry of "Lord Jesus Christ, Son of God, have mercy on me". Under no circumstances give yourself any rest.'

Gregory Palamas was in dispute with Barlaam of Calabria, whom he criticized for preferring the more rationalizing Western style of theological activity. In return, Barlaam criticized Gregory and the Hesychasts for Messalianism, a heresy with charismatic tendencies fashionable from the fourth to the seventh centuries, which questioned the necessity of the sacraments. It could even accommodate a degree of dualism, in the form of the idea that successful prayer transformed the body and made it more spiritual. The Synod of Constantinople of 1368 adopted Palamas as a Father and Doctor of the Church, thus setting an Eastern seal of approval on his approach and emphasis.

The question of the relation of heresy and schism to orthopraxis has not died away altogether. In the era of the popularity of 'liberation theology' in Latin America the challenge to the centrality of historical Western priorities and cultural assumptions was the call for a newness of Christian life, a willingness to bring forward the needs of the poor.[19]

So the important threat inherent in the breakdown of a common order was that of schism. Only when disputes about order divided Christians did they become serious. These examples indicate how hard it can be to separate lapses from the one faith from breakdowns of the common order. We must consider next the complexities which have clouded attempts to 'classify' heresies, many of which arise from this difficulty.

Chapter 4

Classifying Heresies

Christianity has always had to find a means of expression within the language of a particular time and place. This has meant not only translation of its teaching from one actual language to another, but also its transfer from one set of cultural assumptions to another. In the first Christian centuries, there was a need to establish how Christian doctrine 'fitted' with existing systems of religious belief in the Greek and Roman world. It was not contentious that it was distinct from the polytheisms of paganism. It was a monotheistic religion which, like Judaism, would have nothing to do with the pervasive syncretism of the Roman world. But it was not so easy to say what made it unlike any other religion.

Heresis had three main senses in early Christian Greek. One took it to mean just a 'way of thought', and that could be used of the Christian faith itself, with no pejorative connotations. In another sense it could mean a system or 'school' of thought, as distinct from a separate community or schism. Its third sense is the one which is important for our purposes. *Heresis* began to be used for a 'false teaching' which purported to be true faith for Christians. Therein lay its danger, for it could mislead the faithful. This evolution of the understanding of what 'heresy' meant underlies many of the difficulties discussed in these pages.

What Could be Imported from Ancient Philosophy?

The first question is how far the Christian faith was independent of contemporary philosophy. Ancient philosophical systems were typically not merely systems of thought. They involved a way of life, too; it is not inappropriate to think of them as 'religions'. There was a running problem throughout the first centuries of deciding what to bring into the discussion of the Christian faith from the world of the philosophers. The schools of philosophy produced much of the sophisticated thought and writing which was the intellectual heritage of Christianity (alongside its debt to Judaism). Yet philosophy was not Christianity because it did not 'know Christ'.[1]

The Hellenistic Jew Philo of Alexandria (d.c.50 AD) had encouraged the use of allegorical interpretations of biblical texts. This was a useful way of showing through imagery how close pagan philosophy sometimes came to the distinctively Christian position. It was risky, though. As a Christian scholar, Origen (c.185–c.254) had developed this method in conjunction with the influence of late Platonism to a point where his ideas verged on unorthodoxy. Yet he wrote a long work *Against Celsus*, the pagan philosopher. As late as Arnobius (late third-early fourth century) this problem of 'suspect orthodoxy' was still visible in authors writing 'against the pagans'[2] He is defensive, and at the same time, on the attack. He has met people who are insane enough to think that the world has gone to pot since there were Christians in it. But is it not rather the reverse, he asks? Surely the world has benefited from the influence of the Christian faith? (I.i.1) For information on the opinions of philosophers Augustine recollects that Celsus is helpful, if not exhaustive.[3]

A special early difficulty was to establish a Christian orthodoxy about the three Persons in one God. Were the three Persons equal or did they form a hierarchy, like the one recognized by the Platonists? Were the three Persons all eternal, or did the Father bring the Son and the Holy Spirit into being in some way which made them subsequent to himself? This was still being clarified in the Latin-speaking world in the time of Augustine of Hippo.

Another area of great difficulty for early Christians, arising in part from the influence of philosophical traditions, was 'dualism', or the separation of matter and spirit into two worlds under two creators. That is the subject of chapter 6.

Incarnation and Christology

Another, closely connected, great issue of the early centuries was what it could mean to say that 'God became man' in Christ. Some believers found it difficult to accept that if he was God, Christ was really human; others were not sure that if he was human, he could also be truly divine. Opposing positions early in the Christian story were those of the Ebionites, who saw Jesus as a merely human Messiah, and the Gnostics, who believed that there was no real assumption of humanity, that the Son of God merely 'appeared' to be human, but remained solely divine. The sheer difficulty of understanding how the highest Being, a God some regarded as above Being itself, could have become a real human being, led to attempts to rationalize or explain or find a convenient image. Some said Christ was merely wearing his humanity like a dress or a cloak. The Arianism which caused huge disturbance to orthodoxy at the beginning of the fourth century belongs in this big group of heresies in that it denies the divine nature of Christ and says that he was merely 'created' by the Father.

In the following centuries variations on this debate continued to provoke strong feeling and to win adherents to schools of thought in vigorous conflict with one another. Nestorius (d.c.451) attacked the use of the word *Theotokos* (God-bearer) by devout Christians to describe the Virgin Mary. He believed this was leading worshippers astray because it encouraged them to think that she was somehow merely a vessel for God's coming into the world, rather than the mother of a real human being who was also God. Insisting on the reality of the human and the divine alike, he held that there were two distinct Persons in the incarnate Christ. The Eutychians are so called after Eutyches of Constantinople (c.378–454), who was anxious to confute what he believed to be the false teaching of Nestorius; but in his eagerness he was seen to have slipped into the opposite heresy, of confusing the two natures in Christ. He taught that the human nature of Christ cannot have been that of a real ordinary man, and that in any case once the incarnation had taken place, there was one nature only.

Early in the sixth century, Boethius wrote a treatise *Against Eutyches and Nestorius*, in which he tried to explore in the Latin language the implications of saying that in Christ there was a union of God and man formed from two natures (*ex duabus naturis*) or 'in two natures' (*in duabus naturis*). Eutyches was condemned at the Council of Chalcedon of

451, and those Churches, later known as 'Oriental Ortho-dox', which adhered to his teaching after its formal condemnation became known as the Non-Chalcedonian Churches. They are also known as the 'Monophysite' Churches. In this way, 'Monophysitism' (one-natureness') derives in turn from the line of teaching associated with Eutyches. These churches include the Copts, the Syrians and the Armenians. The lingering aftermath of these debates has kept these churches in a state of separation from the Roman Catholic and Orthodox churches ever since.

It was realized after the Council of Chalcedon that the divisions were serious and that it was important to try to mend them. Monothelitism was a seventh-century heresy which took its origin in part from an attempt to reunite the Non-Chalcedonians with the Chalcedonians. The reasons were partly political: in the face of a military threat to the Christian world from Mohammedan invasions it was more important than ever for Christians to be united. A formula was suggested which would recognize that there were two natures in Christ, the divine and the human, but allow only one *energia* or 'source' of his acts. One this proposed solution reached the West, however, it encountered the problem of the growing language barrier between the Greek-speaking East and the Latin-speaking West. The key word *energia* was rendered inappropriately into Latin as 'will', and the Church found that it had a fresh heresy on its hands, suggesting that Christ had two wills.

The truth is that these are not easy doctrines to get clear in any language, nor concepts which it is possible to hold in the mind without a good deal of sophistication and hard thought. Christians today may well find that they have, without knowing it, been Arians or Nestorians or Eutychians or Monothelites and that they could not readily state their faith in Christ in terms the Church through the ages would accept as orthodox.

The Augustinian Trio

In Augustine's lifetime three main problems presented themselves. The first was the threat from the dualists of his own day, the followers of Mani or Manichees (see chapter 6). They taught, like other dualists, that matter is evil and spirit is good; that there are two ultimate powers in the universe, of good and evil. Augustine was an adherent of this sect for nearly a decade, and although he eventually lost confidence in their ability to give him answers to the problem of evil which was troubling him, he never quite shook off the influence of their ideas. Augustine shows himself well aware of their prominence in his *Retractations*, written near the end of his life, in which he goes over his writings, considering what he has written (and, in the main, approving of it). 'I could not be silent about Manichees after my baptism', he comments.[4]

The second was the great schism in north Africa occasioned by the refusal of the Donatists, or followers of Donatus, to accept the ministerial succession of the Catholic Church there. They said Caecilian, who was consecrated Bishop of Carthage in 311, could not be a real bishop because he had been consecrated by Felix of Aptunga, who had abandoned his faith at the time of the persecution of Christians under the Emperor Diocletian (see p.00). This created a crisis about which was the 'true Church', and worried believers could find themselves uncertain whether their hopes of heaven were being diminished by belonging to the wrong party. Augustine made up verses to assist in the memorization of the errors of the Donatists and wrote a good deal on the subject.

The third problem was the pastoral danger presented by the Pelagians, who were influenced by the British preacher Pelagius to think that the imitation of Christ was simply a matter of trying hard to follow his example. Augustine was concerned that people would discount the need for divine assistance (grace). His own view, from personal experience, was that human beings are so profoundly affected by 'original sin', the sin of Adam, that it is impossible for them to be good by their own efforts. They need God's help and they need the support of the Church and its sacraments.

The Easter Controversy

A surprising amount of divisiveness was occasioned by the 'Easter Controversy' which came to a head during the centuries after the end of the antique world. Some Christian festivals are on fixed days of the year. Christmas (except in the Orthodox world) is always on 25 December. Others follow a variable pattern. The timing of Easter each year depends on that of the Jewish Passover, for it was the Passover meal which Jesus ate with his disciples immediately before his arrest and crucifixion. So Easter is one of the 'moveable feasts'. The date of the feast of Ascension 'moves' with Easter. Easter will not be celebrated on the same day by all Christian communities unless they are using the same method of calculation to arrive at the date. Augustine notes (Letter 23) that in 387 Easter was celebrated on 14 March in Gaul, on 18 April in Italy and on 25 April in Alexandria.

The process of establishing any date so as to arrive at a commonly acceptable result was in its infancy until Bede worked out a method in the face of the conflicting usages of the churches in England. This derived from the fact that those won to Christianity by the Celtic mission were celebrating Easter on one date during the seventh century, while those established in the faith by the mission from Rome, led by St Augustine of Canterbury, used another day. The difference caused social conflict, even conflict in the royal household. Famously, the Roman Christian Queen of King Oswy of Northumbria (of Celtic persuasion) kept Palm Sunday in 651 on the day the King celebrated Easter. Theodore, Archbishop of Canterbury, succeeded in bringing the whole of England into conformity on a single date only in 669.

The real importance of these seemingly trivial differences was that the fact that they made the Church appear 'divided' in its celebration of the most important feast of the Church's year. The matter presented itself at the time not as a minor difference over the calculation of dates, but as a schism.

The Doctrine of Transubstantiation

In the late eleventh century, Berengar of Tours became prominent as an individual who would not be silent. He wanted to clarify exactly what happened when a priest took bread and wine and said Christ's words at the Last Supper, 'This is my body' and 'This is my blood'. This was a matter which proved to be of central importance to orthodoxy once he had focused attention on it. By the end of the controversy Berengar began there was a doctrine of transubstantiation, which asserted that the rules of Aristotle's *Categories* were reversed. Whereas ordinarily bread changes in appearance as it grows mouldy but remains still in substance bread, in the case of the consecrated bread its appearance remained exactly the same, but in its substance it became literally the Body of Christ.

The doctrine of transubstantiation devised in response to the challenge from Berengar became settled and accepted by the end of the twelfth century (the time when it acquired its label of 'transubstantiation'). It did not, however, bring to an end controversies about the Eucharist, but they were to shift ground. The insistence that the bread and wine truly became the physical body and blood of Christ altered in the fifteenth century to a preoccupation with the rather more subtle idea of his 'real presence'. In the early sixteenth century the Protestant reformers began to argue against the sacrificial character of the Eucharist, because they said that this teaching detracted from the uniqueness and completeness of the sacrifice Christ had made when he died on the Cross. But these new emphases and concerns did not altogether obliterate discussion of transubstantiation. The Council of Trent reaffirmed the doctrine and it was expressly rejected by leading reformers such as Luther and Zwingli.

1054 and the Schism of East and West

After the fall of the Roman Empire, a language division and a division of style of thought divided the Empire into two parts, as the numbers in the West who could speak Greek diminished and the numbers of Greeks with adequate Latin became correspondingly small. The tension is visible in Augustine. He found Greek difficult and struggled to make Latin an adequate vehicle in which to explain those clarifications of Trinitarian and Christological questions which had been arrived at by the Council of Nicaea after all the disputes among Greek speakers during the Arian controversy. So much depended, as the creation of the 'Monothelite heresy' showed, on a nuance which might not 'translate'. The problem therefore goes much deeper than a relative unfamiliarity with another language. There were also contrasts in philosophical style which made the heritage of Neo-Platonism in the West a very different thing from its later history in the East, where more mysticism attached to it.

The Greek East had an 'Iconoclast Controversy' (see p.39) at a period when there was no real anxiety on this subject in the West, certainly not enough to prompt the internal warfare and cries of mutual condemnation it occasioned in the East.

The *Filioque* clause was added to the Nicean Creed in the West in the Carolingian period. The clause 'Who proceeds from the Father and the Son' originally read 'Who proceeds from the Father'. The addition caused great offence in the Eastern half of mediaeval Christendom, because the Greeks would not allow any change to the original formulation. Their objection seems to have been more to the innovation than to the substance of the addition itself, though both became matters of fierce controversy for many centuries after 1054, when the two halves of Christendom became divided, partly as a result of a political squabble, but with long-lasting consequences for the unity of the Church. The division is still not mended.

But there was of course much more at stake. The Greeks objected that the addition radically altered the doctrine of the Trinity, creating 'two first principles', Father and Son, from whom the Holy Spirit somehow derives, and undermining the core doctrine that God is one by suggesting that he is somehow 'two'.

Anselm of Canterbury was asked by the Pope at the Council of Bari in 1098 to explain to the Greeks who were present there why the Western view was 'right'. He also wrote on another of the topics on which division had been 'justified', the question of whether leavened or unleavened bread should be used in the Eucharist. The West insisted on unleavened bread, the East on bread with yeast in it. While defending the Western usage, Anselm said that it did not matter. Both were bread and that was the important point.

The final, and major, area of disagreement between East and West was over the 'universal primacy'. It will be recollected that, since early Christian times, there had been several 'patriarchates' or senior bishoprics, at Jerusalem, Antioch and Rome, at Alexandria and latterly at Constantinople. Rome made its claim to be first.

Anselm, Bishop of Havelberg, went to Constantinople in the mid-twelfth century and held 'ecumenical conversations' with Greek Christian leaders there to try to mend the schism. His *Dialogues* reporting the inconclusive results still survive. They show how far apart the 'mindset' of East and West had now grown as Anselm wrote his account in Latin for the Western readers who would understand 'Western' assumptions best. He could do no more. The 'common mind' was gone, not only in the sense of a shared view on a matter of faith, but also in the deeper sense of a common approach, a common set of assumptions.

The most significant 'official' attempt to resolve the difference of opinion between East and West was the Council of Florence, which was held in a series of Italian cities, Ferrara, Florence and Rome, between 1438 and 1445. The Patriarch of Constantinople came, and Bessarion, Archbishop of Nicaea, Mark of Ephesus, and many of the leading theologians from the East were present. Bessarion achieved something in tune with twentieth-century ecumenical method, in his *Dogmatic Discourse*. He tried to show that the East and the West had always really taught the same thing. There was even a provisional agreement on the part of the Greeks to accept the Pope as universal Primate.

The agreement foundered, however, when the eastern Bishops took it home and put it to their local synods. The Greek churches 'on the ground' did not recognize the proposals as their own. There was a significant 'structural' reason why the agreement of the Council of Florence did not mend the schism between the Greek East and the Latin West. In the West, the Bishop of Rome as Pope was head of the whole structure, but in the East each of the ancient Patriarchs (Antioch, Alexandria, Constantinople, Jerusalem) led an 'autocephalous' section of the Church. Although these patriarchates agreed in one faith they were self-determining in many ways.

This has proved to be a common phenomenon in more recent 'ecumenical dialogue'. Those involved in trying to reach agreement gain one another's confidence and recognize all sorts of subtleties as a result of talking hard and cooperatively, but those who have not been involved find it difficult to enter into what has happened and 'own' the result. So when the synods said they would not accept the outcome of the Council of Florence this great mediaeval ecumenical experiment failed.

From Sect to 'Confessional Identity'

Some groups of believers in every generation have become formally separated from the Church, claiming that they were in fact the true Church. They have tended to develop a sense of an identity peculiar to themselves, distinguishing themselves from other Christians on some key point. Yet when at the end of the Middle Ages, the Church in the West was faced with numerous 'protestant' breakaway groups the whole scene altered. For the last few hundred years there have been 'Churches', not all recognizing one another by any means, but nevertheless forming in the eyes of many Christians plural ecclesial entities. The World Council of Churches, formed in the twentieth century, captures in its title this change of assumption.

The word *secta* was actively current in a series of patristic authors, for groups who were not *catholici*. The term is the Latin counterpart of the Greek *heresis*.[5] Augustine refers to the *secta manicheorum*. He also speaks of a *secta perversa* which is *contra ipsam catholicam*.[6] Gregory of Tours speaks of the *Arriana secta*.[7] Bede also speaks of the *secta manicheorum*.[8]

There is a strong tradition of identifying a *secta* by the school of thought it represents. It constitutes a choice of viewpoint, as in Augustine's reference to the *sadducaei* as a *secta* of the Jews 'which did not believe in resurrection'.[9] A *secta*, Isidore says, is so called because of the way it follows and holds on to opinions.

But there is also the underlying idea of a separateness which has more to do with 'gathering' as a 'group apart'. The early fifth century Orosius emphasizes this 'gatheredness', but as something which can be taken to constitute a sect even where there is no unity of belief.[10] This is in keeping with Isidore's further definition that a sect is so called because it is like a 'section'.[11]

It was this drawing apart to constitute themselves a superior kind of Christian which Wyclif so disliked about religious orders in the later Middle Ages. Wyclif says there are really only two 'sects', that of Christ and that of worldly men, but he subdivides the class of the wordly into monks, canons and friars. The encouragement of diversity in the religious life is also an encouragement to quarrelling and division, he says. The sects divide the Christian community and thus the unity of Christ's order. Christ wanted his people to be one, as he and his Father are one (John 17.11–9). The divine purpose was that there should be one faith and one baptism.[12] Wyclif's hostility to monks and friars was very powerful. It was driven – or at least rationalized – in terms of the criticism that they laid claim to be more perfect that other Christians; that they had drawn apart into a 'private' religion, excluding other Christians; that this was unscriptural and 'man-made' (that is, not from God); that it was a 'novelty'.[13] But the key objection was the claim to perfection. Separateness alone may create a *secta*, but Wyclif's particular objection is to a separateness which excludes the ordinary run of Christians and seeks to set itself above them. Wyclif identifies as a 'sectarian' error the following of a human leader rather than Christ.[14]

This raises the important question of 'confessional identity' as a means of 'fixing' the position of a group of believers by their own agreed statement. This went beyond the phenomenon found in the late Middle Ages, where groups of Lollards might share a common life in the sense that they would follow the same trades, live in a 'ghetto' and marry only among themselves. The point of distinctive belief might be bizarre. It was reported that William Wakeham of Devizes (1434) thought the earth stood above the sky; John Woodhull of Hereford (1433) held that the worst deed of a man are better than the best deed of a woman.

The adoption of a particular set of ideas or beliefs in a 'confession of faith' gives a group an 'identity' which can be very persistent. The Augsburg Confession was composed in 1530, mainly by Luther's friend Melanchthon and on the basis of earlier confessions of this group of reformers. It was presented to the Emperor Charles V as a coherent statement of the Lutheran position. The 'Lutheran position' thus became clear to 'Lutherans' as well as to their enemies. The Confession won support outside Lutheran circles. For example, Calvin later signed it.

It begins with 21 articles setting out the essentials of the faith as Lutherans saw them, and continues into a list of the abuses which the Lutherans wanted to see corrected. It is in many respects an eirenic document, not in intention divisive. Article 7 describes the Church as the place where the Gospel is preached and the sacraments administered according to the Gospel:

> For it is sufficient for the true unity of the Christian Church that the gospel be preached in conformity with a pure understanding of it and the sacraments be administered according to the divine Word. It is not necessary for the true unity of the Christian Church that ceremonies, instituted by men, should be observed uniformly in all places.

The Lutherans saw the visible Church as a 'mixed' body, in which good and wicked individuals are to be found side by side. It is a community of faith; it has certain 'notes' or 'marks', which are the traditional 'marks of the Church' (one, catholic, holy and apostolic). This Church has authority to condemn heresies, but the Lutherans recognize heresies in different places from those in which the Catholics of the day find them. They condemn the Catholic Church itself because they say it has Antichrist reigning within it.

The Emperor gave this 'Confession' to a committee of Roman Catholic theologians, who set about refuting it. The document began a debate which went on for some decades. The Augsburg Confession in more or less its original form retained its authority for Lutherans.

It became a common practice, especially in the sixteenth century, for Churches defining their positions in opposition or challenge to set out a list of 'articles' in this way. The Thirty-Nine Articles of the Church of England are an example.

The Power of a Name

Some heresies have had identifiable leaders or heresiarchs. Justin (c.155) says in his *Apology*[15] that after Christ ascended into heaven the evil demons sent forth false teachers, including Marcion, leader of the Marcionites, who denied that God the Father made the universe. Isidore too notices that some groups of heretics are called after their initiators. For example, he says that the Simoniaci are called after Simon Magus.[16] A number of individuals became famous leaders of heretical opinion, whose personal powers of leadership or of inspiring their followers – sometimes their sheer notoriousness – were perhaps as important as their ideas in winning them a following. The Arians are called after Arius, priest of Alexandria, says Filastrius. Then there are the 'half-Arians' (Semiarians), who believe correctly about the Father and the Son that they are of one substance, and one divinity, but they hold that the Holy Spirit is a created spirit and not of the divine substance.[17]

Arius did indeed, as Filastrius says, give his name to the Arian controversy. The sixth century *Historia Tripartita* describes 'how Arius arose against the Church' (*contra ecclesiam*). At a time when the Church was flourishing, it explains, the Enemy made a plan. He could see that paganism was a lost cause, so he made war on God and our Saviour. 'I shall describe how this began and how the Enemy sowed weeds', promises Theodoret, who is the source of this passage.[18] The *Historia Tripartita* explains that Arius was a priest in Alexandria who began to claim that there was a time when the Son of God did not exist.[19] The offence lay not only in the heresy involved but also in the schismatic tendency of this teaching to break the 'chain of unanimity and peace in the Church', in other words, to cause schism.[20] More, 'wicked men' (*viri iniqui*) began to teach apostasy to the point where they could rightly be suspected of being forerunners of Antichrist.[21] Arius thus became demonized by the resulting personal prominence.

The historical reality is probably rather different. When it all began, in 318, Arius was respected by the Bishop of Alexandria as a leading exegete. Epiphanius recognized his personal charm. He was 'easily able to deceive any unsuspecting heart . . . He spoke gently; people found him persuasive'.[22] Yet a politically directed set of expectations was at work here. There were social as well as theological forces in what was happening. This created a near certainty that Arius and his following would be condemned at the Council of Nicaea in 325. Arius was accused of saying of Christ that 'before he was begotten he was not', and that 'by his own power the Son of God is capable of evil and goodness', and calling him 'a creature and a work'.[23] These are crude summaries of questions of immense philosophical and linguistic complexity, on which in reality the Church was just forming its view. The letter of the Council to the Egyptians says that 'the affair of the impiety and lawlessness of

Arius and his followers was discussed in the presence of the most pious Emperor Constantine'. It confirms that at that stage it was still not clear what was truly 'catholic' and what was 'Arian' opinion on those subjects.[24]

A century later, when Quodvultdeus (a deacon in Carthage from about 421) and Augustine were corresponding about heretics, it all seemed much clearer. Expounding the creed, Quodvultdeus makes a confident attack on the Arians. 'When you, Arian heretic, hear . . . that the Holy Spirit descended [upon Jesus] in the form of dove, are you not terrified by this authoritative saying?'[25]

In the mid-twelfth century, the priest Peter de Bruys was accused of preaching opinions which undermined order in the Church. He rejected infant baptism and the Eucharist. He argued against prayers for the dead and the veneration of the Cross. He said the Church had no need of buildings. He called on monks to marry. He won a considerable popular following, who were known as the Petrobrusians. In some alarm, Peter the Venerable, the Abbot of Cluny, wrote a book to try to stop this teaching spreading. 'It has travelled, I understand, to places nearby,' he comments. He is consciously writing not only to seek to influence those who were tempted to follow Peter of Bruys, but also to warn good Catholics.[26] This is an example of the mythology not only of active proselytizing but also of long-term 'sleepers', holders of heretical views who lie quiet for many years, ready to lead people astray again when the moment comes. These illustrate the sheer persistence of heresy.[27]

Another figure who became a personal focus of dissident loyalty later still in the Middle Ages was John Wyclif. He had begun as a respected teacher (his teaching career probably began at Oxford in the 1350s) but fell foul of critics who disagreed with his teaching. His contentious views also won him international opprobrium.[28] He too found himself facing the organized opposition of the Church, as we shall see in the next chapter. In 1377 Pope Gregory IX sent bulls to England listing and condemning 19 of Wyclif's 'errors'. Wyclif was driven out of Oxford in the end, in 1381, and spent his retirement as a parish priest at Lutterworth. In 1382 a Council at Blackfriars condemned 10 propositions of his and some of his supporters went into exile for fear of the consequences of being seen to be on his side.

The line of charismatic figures such as Arius and Wyclif turns in the sixteenth century into a line of figures who can be regarded in a quite different light, as the founders of new and enduring ecclesial communities: Calvin and the Calvinists, Luther and the Lutherans, Wesley and the Methodists. Sometimes a continuing ecclesial community has continued in subsequent years and in future generations to call itself after a founder other than Christ. The Lutheran World Federation is an obvious example, even though Lutherans would be more likely to identify themselves as the 'Church of the Augsburg Confession' than as 'Luther's Church'.[29]

Categories of Unbelief

So we see that although from an early stage there were attempts to list and classify the ways in which heresy might manifest itself, it is by no means easy to map the results. This led to groupings which do not always match the broad chronological shifts of emphasis and concern. The great fear was that heresies would return, that they were not finally dispatched when the heretics of the moment were defeated. And of course that is true. The classic unorthodox positions are held in every age by individuals who may not know that they are following in the steps of famous earlier 'heretics', but who have been struck by similar questions.

Augustine wrote a book on the subject very late in his life, in response to a request from Quodvultdeus. He wrote a letter to Augustine asking what to do about heretics who now wished to become Catholics. He was especially concerned about the vexed question of what was to be done about ensuring that they had been validly baptized. No one could be baptized twice, so it was extremely important that the baptismal status of converts from heresy should be clear.[30]

Augustine admits that it is difficult to define heresy. He refers Quodvultdeus to the work of Filastrius Brixensis on this subject and also to that of Epiphanius, who (Augustine thinks) has written in a more learned way than Filastrius.[31] Filastrius grouped types or clusters of heretical error. For example, those who do not practise baptism and those who say angels created our souls and that Christ is not the Saviour are discussed together; there is a separate category for those who dispute the date of Easter; another category contains those who dispute the authenticity of the Gospel of John and the Apocalypse.[32] Filastrius includes a long list of 'Jewish' heresies; he explains that after the death of Christ, Simon Magus and Menander became leaders of heretical thought, and he goes on to detail the patterns of heretical opinion in their historical unfolding.[33] Quodvultdeus struggled with all that. He then wrote back to Augustine, asking for help over the contradictions he perceived between the two authorities to whom he had been referred. Augustine settled down to the writing of a book *On Heresies* for him.[34]

John of Damascus (c.675–749) followed in the same tradition of looking for repeating patterns, in his *On Heresies*, in which he classifies heresies into those of the barbarians, those of the Scythians, 'Hellenisms' and 'Judaeism'.[35]

The difficulty which faced those who wished to classify heresies is illustrated by a passage in Guibert of Nogent's autobiography *On My Life*. In about 1114 he described a leader of heretics living near Soissons called Clement, who was teaching that infant baptism was wrong; he rejected the sacraments in general, including marriage, and his followers were said to indulge in homosexual practices, 'for among them it is unlawful for men to approach women' and 'they reject food of all sorts which are the product of coition'. Guibert goes on, rather confusedly, to accuse them of holding orgies: 'They hold meetings in cellars and secret places, the sexes mingling freely. When candles have been lighted, in the sight of all, light women with bare buttocks (it is said) offer themselves to a certain one lying behind them. Directly the candles are extinguished, they all cry out together "Chaos" and each one lies with her who first comes to hand.' Any children born as a result of these couplings are killed by being 'thrown from hand to hand through the flames by those sitting round the fire'. The dead child 'is then reduced to ashes; from the ashes bread is made, of which a morsel is given to each as a sacrament'. Guibert now contemplates these descriptions and says, uncertainly, 'If you will read the various accounts of heresies by Augustine, you will find that this resembles none more than that of the Manichaeans'.[36]

The problem was that it could be very difficult to say of given individuals or heretics that they were in error, and in what particular respects, when so much went by rumour and association, and when it was easy to add such alleged horrors to the heap of accusations.

Nevertheless, further listings and classifyings of schools of heretical beliefs are not hard to find as the Middle Ages progressed. In the thirteenth century, the former Cathar Durandus provides one, for example, referring to the Manichees, the Nicholaitans, the Passagii, the Speroni, the Runchayroli.[37] Bernard Gui distinguishes five *sectae*: the Manichees, the Waldensians, the Pseudo Apostles, the Beguines, a mixed category of converted Jews who 'return to their vomit', magicians and others.[38]

Numerous labels for groups of heretics or forms of heretical persuasion are to be found. Some of these groups, for example the Passagians – to be found in mediaeval Lombardy and apparently observing Old Testament precepts literally – may have been quite small, and local, but they could nevertheless contribute a strand or preoccupation to the bundle of issues on which there were fears that the Church was being led astray. In short, heresy, especially in the later Middle Ages, came to be looked on not only as an infection, but as a range of symptoms which could be expected to be found together. That applied whether the accusations came from the Church itself or from critics of the Church.

Pinning Accusations to Suspected Heretics

The medieval Inquisition was always looking for a particular stamp, a characteristic set of beliefs, which could safely be take to be indicators of heretical tendencies or full-blown heretical affiliation. This created a tendency for categories and sets of wrong beliefs to be 'pinned' to those whose faith or conformity with order became suspect. Because the Inquisition was often more anxious to identify 'heresy' than to find a particular school of thought in its victims, its questioning might be 'broad brush', going through a series of known points of unorthodoxy, regardless of sect, even 'constructing' the heretic's heresy by means of a particular line of questioning. The approach was analogous with that of a surgeon who seeks to cut out a cancer so that the whole body may survive; the body was the body of Christ.

Raymundus de Costa was repeatedly brought before the Inquisitor Fournier. The question whether he will take an oath is the starting-point, for the refusal to do so could be damning in itself. A resistance to swearing was a common indicator of other dissident opinions. Next Raymundus is taken through the standard issues in which heretics may be expected to be deficient in the faith, but not in a form which would be appropriate only for Waldensians. Some of the questions put to him were designed to search out Cathars. He was required to say that he believed in one God, creator of heaven and earth; citations stating that in the beginning God created heaven and earth, are associated with that, also *'Adorate Eum qui fecit celum et terram'* (Revelation 14.7). That would seem a question more appropriate for a putative dualist, as would the requirement that he affirm that God gave the Old Law to Moses his servant on Mount Sinai (Exodus 24.12).[39] Raymundus was also brought to affirm that he believed in the resurrection of the same bodies as men and women have now (Job 19.25–7), *'et in carne mea videbo Deum'*.[40]

But it was not only the Inquisition which made free with the pinning on of accusations. Prepositinus's *Summa Contra Haereticos*, probably of the late twelfth century,[41] experimented with the grouping of accusations. Wyclif shows in his attacks on the *sectae* the same tendency to aggregate accusations as the ecclesiastical authorities and the Inquisition show in their listing of the errors of heretics. Wyclif accuses the *sectae* of being heretical on the Eucharist, the papacy and priestly power.

As late as the nineteenth century John Henry Newman was still classifying the major types of error in England. In a letter to his mother in 1829,[42] he listed the major types of error which had in his view been found in England: Deists; republicans, utilitarians, schismatics 'in and out of the Church', Latitudinarians, Baptists, and 'the high critics in London'. In his view, these have in common, whether in secular or theological writers, 'a spirit which tends to overthrow doctrine'.

The Creation of a Critical Literature

This by now rather academic attempt to classify heresies thus created a 'critical literature', with a layering of controversy. We noticed that the three major controversies on which Augustine himself wrote a series of books and letters were Pelagianism, Donatism and the Manichees. This created a 'literature' which in its turn became a resource for those who found themselves appraising the issues in other controversies arising perhaps many centuries afterwards. Alan of Lille quotes Augustine a good deal in his four books against the 'heretics' of the late twelfth century.

Aquinas, in the middle of the thirteenth century, was composing a *Summa* 'against the unbelievers' (*Summa contra Gentiles*). His method was to take heresies topic by topic, listing all the ways he knew of believing wrongly about each point of a systematic theology, the existence of God, the nature of God, the Trinity, Incarnation, and so on, and to seek to provide Dominicans with a handy reference manual of answers when they encountered the heresy in question in the mind of a living person.

In the same spirit, John Hus wrote protestingly in defence of Wyclif after his condemnation by the University of Prague in 1403:

> You declared recently that Wyclif is a heretic, for the reason he had written heresy in his books. That does not seem to be a sufficient reason: for then on the same ground the blessed Augustine and many others would be heretics, for in their pronouncements they scholastically posited heresies; as did the master of the sentences, St. Thomas, and others.[43]

An important question with which we are left at the end of this chapter on the bewildering grouping and regrouping of challenges is whether some sets of ideas naturally belonged together or tended to entail one another. The following chapters, on the 'social challenge' posed by the anti-establishment dissidents (chapter 5) and on 'Good and evil' (chapter 6), examine some of the ways in which they seem to have done so.

Chapter 5

Heresy and Social Challenge

Jesus preached a social as well as a spiritual Gospel. He taught his disciples to live simple lives, expressing their love of their neighbours as well as of God (Mark 12.31). This summary of the commandments, ironically, came to be regarded as presenting a potential challenge to the authority of the Church itself. This chapter is mainly about those who were classified as 'heretics' because they tried to take the imitation of Christ seriously.

In the early Church the Christians posed a social threat, not so much through their endeavours to follow Christ in his simplicity of life, but because they would not comply with the contemporary and very different 'social requirements' of the day. They refused to worship the Emperor as a god. They would not merge their worship in the general syncretism in which the pagan gods of the conquered peoples all over the Roman Empire had become mingled. This meant that in the first Christian centuries Christians themselves were outlaws, periodically persecuted by a state which tried to insist that they fell into line with its religious requirements. That was not a problem for pagans. Augustine of Hippo discusses in Book VI of his *City of God* the limitations of the idea of a 'civic religion' which ties religious practice to good citizenship but is little better than simple pagan nature-worship, and is indeed an extension of it.

The ideal of the 'apostolic life' began to come into its own some centuries later, as the hand of late antique philosophy lost its grip on Christianity. Group after group among the mediaeval 'heretics' called for simplicity in following the way of life Jesus taught. They castigated the Church and its clergy and the members of the religious orders for losing sight of what really mattered. Friars Preachers (the Dominicans), says Wyclif disparagingly, squabble with Friars Minor (the Franciscans) about going barefoot; there are more important things to think about in the endeavour to follow Christ.[1] Jan Hus remarks in an early letter: 'I wish therefore . . . that you leave off circumlocution and extraneous glosses, and in true love with Jesus Christ preach the poverty which our Lord and his disciples also taught by word and example'.[2]

On the face of it, it is extraordinary that it should be the heretics whose voices are raised in this way. This was surely what the Church should have been preaching? Nothing could be more fundamental to Christ's teaching than the kind of thing they were saying. Yet they were outlawed for saying it. One reason was the recognition by the Church's authorities that in reality the kinds of people most enthusiastic about taking this teaching literally were also likely to be on the fringes of society. The wealthy and powerful (and by the Middle Ages that included most of those in positions of leadership in the Church), are not likely to be found casting away their possessions with the same enthusiasm as those who have few possessions to abandon.

An exceptional individual might do it. Francis of Assisi is the obvious mediaeval example, and he and his followers won official approval for a time. Yet when he died his 'Franciscans' divided in a bitter feud which drew the whole Church in the West into a 'poverty controversy' lasting some generations. Those who wanted to keep to the foundation principles of the movement, and resist the acquisition of wealth and buildings and the adoption of the institutional structures which seemed to require such possessions, became the outlaws. Those Franciscans who found it convenient to become involved with property became respectable.

This sequence of events illuminates a certain inherent tension in all mediaeval monastic and religious life. Outlaws and outsiders are exactly the people Christ especially encouraged his followers to love. Christ urged his followers not to reject strangers and outcasts; the stranger is a guest to be entertained (Matthew 25.35). To be in exile from the world and on a spiritual pilgrimage was a sign of holiness.

In mediaeval Western Europe, at least from the time of Benedict of Nursia in the sixth century, the religious orders provided a 'safe' and socially respected means of following Christ's lead without appearing a threat to society by detaching oneself from wealth and a respect for material assets. 'Outcasts for God' were thus 'contained'. They were 'held' within the small ordered society of the religious house, under a requirement of stability which in principle prevented their wandering about, under obedience to their superiors, pilgrims in their souls, not their bodies. From countenancing and containing this awkward tendency to set wealth and power at nought, society drew the benefit of the prayer of these dedicated souls.

But the Benedictines became rich and often corrupt as they acquired more and more property. They ran great estates. The Mendicants – Dominican and Franciscan – began as wandering preachers. At first that made them a potentially disruptive influence if they took Christ's call to live the apostolic life too seriously and too simply and literally. The vision of Francis ended with his death. Some of his followers tried to continue, but others were anxious to establish a more formal institutional structure, with the inevitable move towards involvement with property and bids for power. Those who resisted were labelled as a dangerous fringe movement and 'excluded'. A debate on 'poverty' ensued which involved the whole Church. The official conservative Church position which emerged might well have surprised Christ's original Apostles. It was argued, for instance, that Jesus had not seriously meant his followers to be poor, that property need not actually be owned: it could merely be 'used' or 'enjoyed'. Within a generation of their founding at the beginning of the thirteenth century, the Mendicants were competing for the most prestigious professorships in the new universities and acquiring property and influence, just like other 'successful' and 'approved' organs of the Church.

Popular Heresy: The Anti-establishment Dissidents Speak up for Themselves

Although 'popular' heresy (heretical belief held by groups of ordinary people) was to be found in the tenth century,[3] the Synod of Orléans in 1022 seems to have been the first instance of a burning for heresy in the mediaeval West. Almost nothing is known about the details of this significant episode. To the Synod of Arras in 1025 were brought some heretics from Italy. It was said that they were claiming that they alone had the key to the truth; that only in their 'way' could sinners be cleansed of their sin. 'Their way' was the apostolic way, the imitation of Christ.

The surviving description of the manner in which they were examined suggests that to begin with it was possible for the issues popular heretics raised when they questioned authority to be debated publicly and without undue acrimony. Things had not yet reached the point where the very appearance of such a group would trigger strong adversarial reactions, where they would be automatically 'classified' and condemned. There was apparently serious and quite open-minded discussion of the merits of what they were saying. It was admitted that they did not accept the sacraments. They were asked how, in that case, they answered the words of Jesus to Nicodemus, when he told him that no one could enter the Kingdom of Heaven unless they had been born again of water and the spirit (John 3.5). They answered that their 'law and discipline' did not seem to them to be contrary to the Gospel or to 'apostolic sanctions'. They explained that they tried to follow the apostolic way of life, abandoning the world, restraining fleshly appetites, harming no one and loving their neighbours.

They said that those who lived in that way had no need of baptism; for those who did not live such lives, baptism could be of no avail. They described this as their *justificationis summa*, the essence of their doctrine of justification. Baptism can add nothing to it. Baptism, they said, had served its purpose in the history of the Church, and was no longer needed.[4] There is much in this exchange about which we should like to know more, for example, the degree of 'writing up' to which it has been subjected by the clerks who made the record of the proceedings of the synod. It is a recurring problem in the case of popular heresies where there is no leader such as a Wyclif or Hus who leaves a proper account of himself with his own pen, that the record is subject to the tidying up of the views of heretics by those not necessarily in sympathy with their views. Nevertheless, even in the form in which we have it, this is a helpful indicator of the consistency and core principles of an ideal which was still to be recognizably there at the heart of the dissident movement which emerged more than a century later under the leadership of Waldes of Lyons. For almost all those of the 'anti-establishment' type seem to have had in common a desire to live the apostolic life, to follow the Jesus of the New Testament.

These early recorded debates took place before the period of the Inquisition when such apparent open-mindedness and willingness to listen on the part of the Church's enquirers seems largely to have vanished. They seem to represent a real debate, with the official Church genuinely trying to establish what the people brought before them to have their opinions examined really believed and taught. Nevertheless, alleged heretics from among the general population of the largely illiterate and uneducated, expected to answer for themselves before a bishop or his representatives, would be faced with theologians' questions, because no one knew how else to explore with them what they had been saying. They would naturally find such questions difficult to answer.

The situation, as the 'accused' faced the local church authorities, might be compounded by factors which had nothing to do with religious belief. There were social and political aspects, such as the formation of alliances between the powerful local laity, even the nobility, to 'support' or 'condemn' such groups or the heretical cliques. Something of the sort seems to have happened in the case of heretics in the region of Albi in the late twelfth century. This was the part of Languedoc where the Albigensian heresy was to be concentrated. The Bishop of Albi and leading churchmen met spokesmen for the villagers of Lombers.

The Acts of the Council of Lombers in 1165 record the questions the leaders of the alleged heretics were asked. First came the question about which parts of Scripture they accepted. This was a test for dualism (see chapter 6). The reply was that, broadly, they accepted the New Testament but not the Old. They were then asked to describe their faith. They refused. They were asked about their baptismal practice. Did it include infant baptism? This they would not answer either, but they expressed themselves willing to answer questions on the Gospels and Epistles.

Once more an attempt was made to get them to describe their faith, by asking them about the Eucharist. They said that it made a difference whether those who participated received the consecrated bread 'worthily' or in the wrong spirit. They said that any good man, whether or not he was a priest, could consecrate the bread. Then they refused to say more on the grounds that they were not willing to answer questions about their faith. Questioned on marriage and penance they cited the relevant New Testament authorities and were silent.

But they found it difficult to stick consistently to this policy. 'They also made many unsolicited statements. They affirmed that they should not swear any kind of oath', and they spoke out against corrupt and wealthy clergy. The outright challenge to authority was too much. The bishop then condemned them as heretics. 'The heretics retorted that the bishop who delivered the sentence was a heretic, not they; that he was their enemy; that he was a ravening wolf, a hypocrite, an enemy to God.' Now they declared their faith readily enough, addressing themselves to the 'whole people' who made up the audience of this 'hearing'.[5]

Another example of genuine attempt at debate (where the heretics were unwilling to play the game), is recorded for Vézelay in 1167. Some heretics known as 'Publicans' were arrested and, when they were examined, they were evasive. They were put into solitary confinement for at least 60 days, to await a hearing. At intervals they were brought out to face their accusers. They 'were frequently brought before the gathering and questioned – now with threats and again with soft words – about the Catholic faith. At length, after the expenditure of much effort . . . they were adjudged guilty of the charge.'

In fear of being burned, two of the heretics recanted and said that they accepted the faith of the Church. They were 'tried' by the ordeal of being plunged into water, to test whether their repentance and conversion was genuine, according to whether they drowned or floated. This practice (ended soon after this date), relied on a supernatural signal to tell human judges whether someone was guilty. The idea was that it must be quite clear to God whether these individuals remained heretics or were now true Catholics. On the other hand, God was not to be 'put to the test'.

One of the two in this case was cleared by the water ordeal; in the case of the other, the verdict was uncertain. After a 'retrial' he was ordered to be burned, but the abbot intervened and changed the sentence to a public flogging. The others, however, were burned.[6]

It is clear from these examples that conscientious Christians could easily find themselves in trouble for simply trying to follow what they thought the Church was teaching. An example of the dangers of simple straightforwardness in taking it seriously when the Church seemed to be calling for reform was the debate about simony (buying ecclesiastical office) and clerical celibacy in the eleventh century. In the East priests were allowed to marry, although it was expected that monks would be celibate. In the West, despite some attempts to insist on clerical celibacy, it was common for priests to have mistresses and children. That was leading to simony, as priests understandably sought to provide for their children by 'handing on' their benefices. There were serious efforts to curb this practice at the end of the eleventh century, with some degree of success, for it ceased to be acceptable for priests to have 'families'. This was one aspect of the broader problem of the attempt to buy ecclesiastical preferment, which could take many forms.

A twelfth-century chronicle describes events in the late 1070s when a bishop travelling through a village was told of a local heresiarch. On the face of it this was an individual doing no more than taking the Church's call for reform at its face value. The man in question, Ramihrdus, was said to be 'laying down doctrine not consonant with the faith' and to have many disciples. He was brought before the bishop and examined on his faith, 'but in all things he avowed the precepts of the true faith'. However, when the bishop put him to the test by asking him to receive the consecrated bread at the Mass he refused, 'asserting that he would take it from none of the abbots or priests, not even from the bishop himself, because they were all deeply involved in the crime of simony or other greedy practice'. He was burned as a heretic.[7]

That was not the end of this maintaining of a double standard in a Church committed to the ending of simony but not eager to hear from protesters and reformers saying the same thing in ways which were critical of the reality of the way the clergy were allowed to live. In his 'two kinds of heretics' at the end of the fourteenth century, Wyclif distinguishes the simoniacal, among whom he includes pope, bishops and curates, and the apostates, among whom he includes all priests who refuse to follow the humble example of Christ.[8]

The Waldensians

From the twelfth century there grew up a series of dissident groups with a popular following, of which the first of real importance was that of the Waldensians. They were to maintain with a degree of consistency the kinds of positions just touched on. Their faith on the points set out in the ancient creeds was on the whole orthodox, but they challenged the Church's teaching on matters of 'order'. In particular they disputed the need for people to fulfil the requirements imposed by the systems of sacraments and ministry if they were to get to heaven. In effect, they were asking whether individual Christians could not hope for heaven just as well if they simply put their faith in God. They disturbed the Church's leaders because they were seen as a threat to their authority, and to the by now immense and complex system of wealth and power through which that authority was exercised.

Plate 4 Waldensian community of Dormillouse in the French Alps, engraving from William Beattie, *The Waldenses, or Protestant valleys of Piedmont, Dauphiny and the Ban de la Roche* (London, 1838). British Library, London.

The Waldensians included articulate townspeople, some of whom were not wholly ignorant of theology or the Bible. Such members of the early mediaeval bourgeoisie began to be able to make themselves heard, as a class, from the eleventh and twelfth centuries, even though they were not clerics and lacked formal education. It is no coincidence that Waldes of Lyons is a prominent example. A transforming moment of insight showed him the way to live as a Christian and he set about acting upon it. At first he did not meet opposition. His project even recommended itself to the local clergy. Étienne de Bourbon says that he turned to two priests for guidance, one of whom, Stephen d'Anse, translated some portions of the Bible (now lost), notably the Gospels and the Psalms, into Lyonnais, a dialect of Provençal. Waldes himself preached, especially on passages from the New Testament. He founded a lay community, who read the Bible and prayed together and confessed to one another.[9] Women were often active in such groups, and played an equal part with men in some groups' activities. They went about in pairs, of mixed sexes, preaching the Gospel.

The oldest surviving documentary evidence from within the movement may be as late as 1230, by which time Waldensian ideas were different and more 'politically' radical than those which had first fired Waldes.[10] There is a 'confession', preserved in the Decretals of Pope Gregory IX. This may give a picture of the early position of Waldes, though to judge from the evidence of a remark of the commentator Ermengaud, it may represent what he found he 'had' to say rather than what he may have wished to say. Ermengaud says that Waldes swore before a cardinal of the Roman Church that he had never held the views of this sect nor associated with its members.[11] The 'confession', together with a list of points condemned, reappears in a letter of Innocent III in 1208, in which he writes to the Bishop of Tarragon asking him to receive the newly converted Durandus,[12] a former Waldensian who had returned to the Catholic fold.

Durandus of Huesca was himself for a time a Waldensian. He wrote an *Antiheresis* at a time in which he argues against both Cathars and Catholics. Durandus was converted back to orthodoxy at Pamiers in 1207, and then became Prior of the Poor Catholics, an order which was, perhaps surprisingly, in view of his 'history', able to obtain papal approval for its members to engage in preaching without diocesan control.[13] But it was not to operate without papal control. Innocent laid down careful rules. The group was to remain 'beneath the rule and authority of the Roman Pope'. It was to take neither silver nor gold in payment for its preaching; its members were to undergo instruction by those who had a knowledge of Scripture and the points to be made in arguing with heretics so as to bring them back to the faith and into the bosom of the Holy Roman Church. Those members not equipped to take part in this work were to stay quietly at home, living holy lives.[14] Durandus became, in effect, a professional controversialist and his writings afford an unusual depth of insight into the development of the ideas of the Waldensians. From this time we have in this rather older Durandus a former Waldensian who is writing against the Cathars, a writer who was once an anti-Establishment heretic taking issue with the dualists with the zeal of a convert.[15] Nevertheless, many of his points remained much as he had made them in his earlier work, and that is indicative of the immense amount of common ground there was between these 'socially aware' heresies.

Durandus's own 'confession' is an expanded creed, with particular emphases in areas where the Waldensians were being asked to make it clear that they were not dualists. For example, 'we believe that the Old and the New Testament had the same author, who created all things, and who sent John the Baptist'. There are also elements to which Waldes and his followers perhaps found it more difficult to assent in later years. The confession asserts that no one can be saved (*extra quam neminem salvari credimus*), outside the one holy, catholic and immaculate Church; it accepts baptism for the remission of sins; confession to a priest as 'according to Scripture', *secundum scripturas*; the 'real presence' of Christ in the consecrated elements of the Eucharist. It promises obedience to the precepts of the 'evangelical Councils'.[16] Resistance on a number of these points became issues of principle for the Waldensians in later years, after they had been excluded from the Church.

At first Waldes had no wish to be outside the fold and in 1179 he won approval from the Third Lateran Council. This Council made a series of pronouncements designed to discourage corruption in the Church and especially among its clergy. It condemned Publicani and Patarenes and Cathars (Canon 27). But it did not condemn the Waldensians, even though they apparently did not put up a good performance as amateur theologians when questioned by the Council. The contemporary commentator Walter Map describes the way the Waldensians were made to look foolish when questioned on theological points.[17] Nevertheless, the Pope gave them authority to preach so long as they did so with the approval of local clergy. Waldes obediently came before the diocesan synod at Lyons in 1180, and signed a profession of faith so that he and his followers might continue to preach with formal local approval.[18] In many respects, preaching as 'wanderers', and living on alms, the Waldensians at this date foreshadowed the mendicant orders, which were to gain papal approval in 1215.

But these genial and permissive circumstances abruptly changed. The tension between charism and order, independent and 'authorized' ministry, always close to the surface, soon emerged as a real difficulty. John Bellesmains became archbishop and in 1182 Waldes and his followers were told to stop preaching. This was a defining moment. Faced with challenge, Waldes said that he must obey God, not man. In continuing to preach when permission had been withdrawn, he did the one thing which would in the end inevitably make him unacceptable to the Church, and turn him into an outlaw, however well he preached and however helpful the content of his preaching to the salvation of the faithful. The archbishop expelled him from the diocese. At the Council of Verona 1184, Pope Lucius III condemned the Waldensians, along with others who preached with a similar disregard for the need to get an official licence. The Waldensians scattered, and continued their work.

Heresy, successfully resisting the Church's censure and carrying on regardless, became schism. Groups such as the Waldensians and the Humiliati, north Italian wool workers living lives of charitable work (and also condemned at Verona), ceased to set a good example when they continued with their work without the Church's official support and against its orders.

The Church remained open for a short time yet to the notion that the 'apostolic life' movements were a potential influence for good in the Church. The clergy were being censured by Councils for their failure to follow Christ's example. Here were preachers with the right priorities. But it was important that the Church should be in control of such 'movements'. The Fourth Lateran Council, as late as 1215, was prepared to give official sanction to Dominicans and Franciscans, but that was on the understanding that they were being 'sent' by the Church. The 'sending' was essential. In its third Canon the Fourth Lateran Council takes a firm line on heretics in general, but especially on those who, 'holding to the form of religion but denying its power' (2 Timothy 3.5), take it upon themselves to preach (*auctoritatem sibi vendicant praedicandi*). St Paul, is cited, asking 'How shall they preach unless they are sent?' (Romans 10.15).[19] In supporting the Dominicans, Innocent III was 'sending' them. He saw the possibility of a worldwide order of preachers, who would work for the Church and under its authority.[20] The reasons for the Church's shift to disapproval of the Waldensians were perhaps much the same as those which prompted its resistance to the similar 'call to be Christlike' on the part of those Franciscans who wanted to go on after St Francis's death in the life of poverty and simplicity he had led in such an exemplary way, and which had attracted a keen following in the first place. For it was also a direct challenge to what had become, with the contemporary aggrandisment to papal claims to plenitude of power, a considerable ecclesial power structure.

When Alan of Lille wrote his fourfold treatise 'Against the heretics' in the late twelfth century, he made a point of this aspect of the Waldensian error. Waldes was 'led by his own spirit, not sent by God' (*suo spiritu ductus, non a Deo missus*). 'He invented a new sect which presumed to preach without the authority of a prelate, without divine inspiration, without knowledge (*sine scientia*), without education (*sine littera*)'. He and his followers say that no one is to be obeyed except God, in particular that only good priests ought to be obeyed. They say that powers to consecrate or bless are not bestowed with ordination; that the faithful may confess to the laity. They say that salvation does not lie in the Church but in living the apostolic life.[21]

The 'offence' of independent preaching, preaching without licence or permission or 'sending', was correctly regarded as the presenting symptom of a militant discontent on other matters. The Waldensians dispersed into the areas in which the Cathars were to be found, south-west France and northern Italy.[22] There were fears in ecclesiastical circles that they would become infected with Cathar views.[23] It is not surprising that there was indeed a resulting degree of overlap in the thinking of the Waldensians and the dualists, heightened by this relegation of the Waldensians to the category of 'outlaw'. Waldensians continued to be active in preaching against the Cathars in the late twelfth century, even after they themselves were banned from preaching.[24] Yet they could not but recognize that they had, in important respects, a common objective with the dualists. They were both striving after the 'perfection' which was often the goal of heretical sects (the Pelagians too). The Waldensians were trying to live perfectly in imitation of Christ; the Cathars had a class of the *perfecti* among their members. There was also a certain parallelism of ascetic practice and ideal.

John Wyclif and the Lollard Movement

John Wyclif (c.1320–84) was an academic whose views first became contentious inside the world of the University of Oxford.[25] He probably began to teach at Oxford in the 1350s. His first writings on logic survive from 1361–71,

Plate 5   John Wycliffe. Private collection.

when he was already making a name. The university world was by now accustomed to public controversy. Oxford itself had long been something of a centre of discontents and challenges. Richard Fitzralph, Thomas Bradwardine and Thomas Buckingham had all been involved in controversy in their day. Richard Fitzralph (at Oxford from about 1315, a Fellow of Balliol before 1325 and Chancellor of the University of Oxford 1332–4 before becoming Dean of Lichfield in 1335), who came to be thought of as a 'Lollard Saint', left a collection of sermons and anti-mendicant writings and something approaching a cult formed. Wyclif was certainly influenced by his thinking on the poverty of Christ, in writing his *On the Poverty of the Saviour*, c.1350–6.

Wyclif was seen to be calling, in the same way as the Waldensians, for a return to the plain apostolic ideals, to a simple following of Christ. His *Postilla super totam bibliam*, which he finished in 1375–6, pointed students of Scripture firmly to the poverty and humility valued in the early Church. The *De Civili Dominio* (1376–8) also includes an emphasis on poverty.

In 1377 Bulls of Pope Gregory IX reached London, in which 19 errors of Wyclif were listed. Pressure to get him condemned mounted in England (where he had made political enemies). In 1378 he published *On the Truth of Holy Scripture* and his *On the Church*; in 1379 *The King's Duty* and *The Pope's Power* appeared, considering respectively the powers of king and pope. These were accompanied by numerous other increasingly polemical works as a 'cornered' Wyclif defended his position. Wyclif was now going further than many of the Waldensians and other anti-Establishment dissidents had done, and questioning the legitimacy of the actions and legislation of 'authorities', whether civil or religious. He argued that Christ had forbidden his followers to exercise civil dominion, so that all ecclesiastical exercise of civil power becomes improper. He now saw such exercise as corrupting.

The controversy on the Eucharist of 1380–1 finally brought about his downfall. William Barton, one of Wyclif's enemies, contrived to get the University to make a public condemnation of Wyclif's teaching. He brought together a 'commission' of 12 doctors for the purpose in 1380, and this brought about Wyclif's ejection from the University.

Wyclif was finally driven out of Oxford in 1380, at the age of about 50, and he lived out his life in retirement at Lutterworth parsonage from 1381. In 1382 a Council at Blackfriars condemned 10 propositions of Wyclif and some of his followers thought it politic to flee the country. Wyclif carried on writing. In 1382 his *Trialogus* was completed and in 1384, the year of his death, the *Opus Evangelicum*.

How did Wyclif, who was himself no great popularizer, and did not seek to communicate his own ideas at a popular level, come to be regarded as the instigator of a popular movement on the scale of Lollardy?[26] He had friends who saw to it that the ideas he had developed by the end of his life were disseminated among lay people. The result was the 'movement' known as 'Lollardy'. Lollardy included ideas familiar from the Waldensians and similar groups of the earlier Middle Ages. For Wyclif's name became associated with an increasingly popular movement, probably during his last years at Lutterworth. His secretary John Purvey did a good deal to encourage this. Nicholas Hereford, Philip Repton and John Aston were also important in spreading Wyclif's ideas. Repton was an Augustinian canon, the others secular clerks. All except John Purvey had been attracted to Wyclif at Oxford and had become fired by him with reforming zeal.

Despite his radical ideas on the Bible, Wyclif was probably not himself the driving force behind the translations of the Bible into English which came to be associated with the Lollards. Nicholas Hereford, a fellow academic who helped to lead the 'Wyclif party' in Oxford in the early 1380s, and John Purvey, who lived in Wyclif's parish and assisted him at the end of his life, have been linked with this translation in its different versions.[27]

Jan Hus

Jan Hus (c.1369–1415) was born in Bohemia.[28] He was ordained priest in 1400, and taught at the University of Prague in the first decade of the fifteenth century. In 1402 he was appointed preacher at the Bethlehem Chapel by the masters of the University. Most of the sermons he preached there survive in Latin (rather than in the Czech in which Hus originally preached them). His sermons encourage people who hear them to lead a good Christian life and use familiar mediaeval methods. He was at first no dissident but a dedicated priest and preacher. 'Have the most just Judge before your eyes, so that you would neither knowingly cause suffering to a just, nor flatter an unjust, man,'[29] he urges in an early letter.

The echoes of the Wycliffite controversy in England reached Hus's Prague. A number of Czechs had been studying in Oxford and events there were known in Prague. There is evidence that Wyclif's own works were reaching Prague by 1390.[30] In 1403 a list of already condemned 'articles of Wyclif' was sent to the office of the archbishop by a disturbed German master, together with 21 'articles' he had added. He asked for an opinion on these. The Czech

Plate 6   Jan Hus, woodcut portrait, Photo AKG London.

masters at Prague (which was divided into 'parties' or 'nations' like many mediaeval universities) saw this as a direct challenge to themselves, for some of them were known to be interested in, even sympathetic to, what Wyclif had been saying. In May 1403 the University of Prague met to consider and condemn as heretical 45 articles said to be derived from the writings of Wyclif.[31]

Hus came in for criticism in the context of the heated debate over Wycliffite and Lollard ideas because he had criticized the rich living of some of the pastors in Prague. There was felt to be a Wycliffite ring to that, and the archbishop received a complaint about him. Hus protested indignantly that he was not preaching against the Church.

In the classic first indignation of the man who subsequently becomes a whistle-blower, he cried:

> I am accused by my adversaries before your Paternity's Grace as if I were a scandalous and erroneous preacher, contrary to the Holy Mother Church, and thus wandering from the faith. . . . With God's help, I wish to refute the scandalous accusations of my enemies laid before your most gracious paternity, humbly and faithfully to give reason for my faith and hope.[32]

When the archbishop ordered that copies of Wyclif's writings which were in the hands of his clergy should be brought to him for 'examination', Hus duly delivered up his own copies.

Hus soon found himself under accusation as a Wycliffite heretic, but he was not without support in the University. The Rector of the University of Prague, Christian of Prachatice, tried to comfort Hus. He cited the assurance in Proverbs 12.21 that nothing which happens to a just man will cause him sadness (*non contristabit iustum quicquid ei acciderit*). In reply, Hus reminded him of 2 Timothy 3.12, which promises that those who try to live a godly life will suffer persecution. He invited Christian to join the battle.

Hus was now caught in the familiar trap of mediaeval 'heretics' and dissidents, from which he could escape neither by 'proving his innocence' nor by 'recantation'. The more vigorously and publicly he defended himself and his orthodoxy the more insistent became the accusations. And, as he attempted to 'explain himself' he was gradually drawn into clearer and clearer statements of positions which began to look very like Wycliffite heresies. He said that God ordered the preaching of his Word throughout the world; that if the Pope and prelates forbid that they are false witnesses; that it is disobedience to God's will which ought to be punished, not the carrying out of his wishes for the ministry of his Word.

In 1411 Hus was excommunicated by the Pope. At the Council of Constance in 1415, he was brought to trial. Peter of Mladonovice, who was an eye-witness and author of some of the documents in play, was a loyal follower of Hus, who shared lodgings with him at Constance. He wrote an account of 'the trial and condemnation of Master Jan Hus in Constance'. So Jan Hus's experience is described at first hand by an observer who had the interests of a lawyer in the implications of some of the documents before the Council.[33]

Hus went to Constance relying on assurances. He still seems to have believed, even when sent for in this way, that if he gave a straightforward explanation of his beliefs the misunderstandings could be cleared up. Peter of Mladonovice emphasizes the openness of Hus's conduct, quoting his letters. 'You should know that I rode openly with an uncovered face'.[34] Hus had agreed to go there under a promised safe-conduct, but he soon found that he was naïve in expecting that he would be given a fair hearing, or a hearing at all. There was even an attempt to try him in his absence.[35]

Hus objected to the fact that he was expected to appear before the cardinals only. He had come on the presumption that he was to render an account to the whole Church assembled in a General Council. 'I have come to the whole Council and there will I say whatever God grants me to say and whatever I shall be asked about'.[36] Against that simplicity the Church brought Didachus, a Spanish minorite friar who behaved like a modern barrister, armed with trick questions.[37]

Peter of Mladovice preserves the record of various dirty tricks which, if these accounts are at all accurate, suggest an 'official' Church in an advanced state of corruption. He overheard a conversation in which it was proposed that Hus should be burned as a heretic even if he did recant. He warned two Czech nobles, Wenceslas of Duba and John of Chlum, that the Council was intending to proceed to its judgement in the absence of the accused. 'If the devil himself came to present his case, he ought to be fairly heard,' he insisted.[38]

There is a dark undercurrent of cynicism in what Mladovice implies about the motivation of Hus's powerful accusers. The rule of *talio* in Roman law was that an accuser who was found to have made false or malicious accusations should be punished by being subjected himself to the punishment which would have fallen on the accused if the case had been proved. Peter of Mladonovice suggests the appropriateness of building in a similar protection for Jan Hus, with his stricture, 'provided they are willing to subject themselves . . . to a like penalty if they do not legally prove against him an obstinate error or heresy.'[39]

The truth was that Hus was entangled in high politics. He had powerful defenders among the influential, and equally powerful enemies, and these leading figures were in reality playing out their own game. Mladovice outwitted the attempt to try Hus in his absence by alerting the Czech nobility. There was interest among them but they complicated matters by condemning the kinds of things which were happening as a result of the row about Hus while seeking to exonerate Hus himself. For example, the petition of the lords of the Czech and Polish nations on behalf of Hus argued that the 'cobblers' who were 'now hearing confessions and administering the most holy body of the Lord to others' were the ones who should be being condemned, not Hus.[40] A trick of his enemies was to associate him with another dubious figure, namely John Wyclif: 'It is stated that the said John Hus obstinately preached and defended the erroneous articles of Wyclif in schools and in public sermons in the city of Prague.'[41] Hus said he had not.

So we see Hus being 'classified' and 'accused' rather than having questions simply and openly put to him so that it might be discovered whether he was truly heretical in his opinions. This is the style of Inquisition rather than of winning back to the fold. Hus was condemned and died at the stake in 1415.

A repeating feature of the thinking of the anti-Establishment dissidents is the way in which the Ministry of the Word comes to stand in opposition to the claims of the Church in its contemporary visible manifestation. Hus began by criticizing priests he knew for living lives which were, as he saw it, unbiblical. He thought he was doing no more than his duty, that he was indeed obeying his

Archbishop. His mistake was not to realize the dangers of criticizing influential people. Hus's ecclesiology, like that of Waldes and Wyclif, was perforce drawn together into a system during the period when he found himself in a position where the enmity of those in power in Church and state alike made it impossible for him to continue to work in Prague. Hus's motivation as a preacher was in the end two-fold: on the positive side, to preach the Word, and on the negative, to preach against 'the malice of Antichrist'. Hus thus saw himself as 'defending the truth' as well as spreading the Gospel.[42]

In exile he was writing a *De ecclesia*, a book on the Church, which he finished in June 1413.[43] In it he crystallized his doctrine of the Church. If the Church is the *congregatio fidelium*, the community of the baptized, it is visible, and Hus had come to believe, as a result of his experiences, that the visible Church had been brought under the control of Antichrist, acting in the persons of the Pope and cardinals. He was concerned not to 'set aside' the Church but to make it clear where the 'true Church' was to be found. If the true Church is the *universitas praedestinatorum*, it is made up only of the elect, it is the mystical body of Christ, it is without spot or wrinkle, it is invisible. The Pope is head of a Church which has ceased to be the true Church. The Church of the elect recognizes the Headship of Christ. Hus wrote to Master Christian of Prachatice from exile some time before April 1413, citing Acts 17.28. It is in Christ that his people live and move and have their being.[44]

For Hus, to say that the Church is the Body of which Christ is the Head meant that it was the whole people of God; it could not consist solely of the cardinals. 'O, if the disciples of Antichrist were content to hold that the holy Roman Church consists of all the faithful, saintly Christians, militant in the faith of Christ'.[45] As it is, he points out, 'it follows that whatsoever the holy Roman Church determines – namely the Pope with the cardinals – that is to be held as the faith.'[46] Hus's teaching thus had much the same ecclesiological implications as that of others identified as 'anti-Establishment dissidents'.

Another natural consequence of the ecclesiology Hus forged in the heat of the controversy which began to surround his teaching was the view that the Word of God itself must be made freely available to all the people of God, and that there must also be freedom for those engaged in the Ministry of the Word. Hus writes to the lords 'gathered at the supreme court of the Kingdom of Bohemia' exhorting them to 'strive to stop' the abuses to which he is drawing attention, 'in order that the Word of God may enjoy freedom among the people of God'. 'I am grieved,' he says, 'that I cannot preach the Word of God, not wishing to have the divine service stopped and the people distressed'.[47]

The Hussite 'Movement'

By the time of Hus's death, the Czech nobility were involved; the battle over Hus had become entangled with high politics and the power struggle between Church and state. Hus became a national hero. His writings gained a lasting influence, especially those of the later period when he had been working out under challenge and threat a body of now quite radical teaching on the nature of the Church. There was now a Hussite 'movement'. During recent centuries a custom had arisen of giving the faithful only the bread at Holy Communion. This probably arose as a matter of convenience at first, but it was resented by reformers who saw in it a statement that priests were 'better' than the ordinary members of their congregations. The Hussites began to offer the ordinary faithful both bread and wine ('Utraquism'), and, perhaps because it was a distinctive mark and easy to fix on, it became a comntroversial 'badge' of the 'movement'.[48]

When leaders of reform die their followers are confronted with the difficulty of deciding whether to carry on, and if they are to carry on, how they are to do it. The history of the Church is full of such moments of decision. They often lead to division and subdivision of the 'movement'. For example, the Franciscans divided after Francis into those who became 'institutionalized' and those who tried to keep alive the flame of the extreme call to poverty they believed to be his legacy; and the Methodists after the death of the Wesleys had to decide whether to strike out and be a 'Church' in their own right.

Hus died a martyr, and in those heightened circumstances another common phenomenon appeared: there were heightened reactions, even that conviction that the end of the world was at hand which has repeated itself throughout Christian history. There was also fragmentation and adoption of extreme positions by some of those who had been, however loosely, of Hus's 'party'. For example, the Taborites, a branch of the Hussite movement who had a fortified 'stronghold' south of Prague called Mount Tabor, were preaching the Second Coming of Christ, and making their own interpretations of the prophetical books of the Old Testament. They spoke of a flight from Babylon, of a gathering of the Elect, of active resistance to the forces of Antichrist. The expected Day of Wrath, when an angry God would descend, failed to materialize.[49] This 'millenarianism' or 'chiliasm' led in the direction of the practices of the Brethren of the Free Spirit, and therefore out towards the 'charismatic fringes' we met in an earlier chapter. It also encouraged people to hand over their worldly goods, in the expectation that they would not be needing them much longer.

The Lollard heresy had begun with academic controversy, and it did not prove difficult for the personal supporters of Wyclif to spread his ideas in a form which caught on very widely among people with no academic pretensions. Something similar happened in the expansion of the Hussite movement, and in the same way a cluster of ideas already associated with Waldes and Wyclif seem to have won ready popular support in the 'Hussite movement'. Taborite priests behaved in a 'Lollard' way, holding services in the open air, without benefit of church buildings or vestments or conventional liturgy. They led worship in the vernacular, and they used rough pieces of bread and any vessel which came to hand instead of a chalice. The authorities responded with a 'witch hunt' against those thought to be Hus's followers.

Social Consequences After the Middle Ages

Social disadvantage to those who, for any of several reasons, were not securely within the fold continued beyond the Middle Ages. The Elizabethan Poor Law in sixteenth-century England expected the poor to remain in the parish where they were born and treated wandering beggars as the enemies of society. The English Test Act of 1673, repealed only in 1829, made it a requirement that everyone who held office under the Crown and, in effect, anyone who was to hold any position of importance in society, should be a member of the Church of England and receive Communion there. It was not until 1871 that Parliament freed academics from a duty to subscribe to the Thirty-Nine Articles of the Church of England.

But these examples underline the importance of the change already touched on. The sixteenth century brought about a Reformation in the West which revolutionized for the future the assumption that there was one visible Church and that to be outside it was to be a heretic or a schismatic. Whereas in the mediaeval West there had been a single Church, from the sixteenth century there were numerous divided ecclesial bodies, not all acknowledging one another as Churches. So it was now possible to be an insider in any of a series of 'Churches' and to regard those in others as 'outsiders'. In the case of the English examples just given, those who 'belonged' socially were members of the Church of England. Others were excluded from social approval as Roman Catholics on the one hand or 'nonconformists' such as Presbyterians or Congregationalists on the other.

Thomas Erastus (1524–83) argued that if a single religion holds sway in a given state, the civil authorities have a right not only to exercise a civil jurisdiction, but also to make decisions in religious matters. The 'Erastian' question arose unavoidably where the Pope no longer held sway. A fragile balance of power between spiritual and temporal had been worked out in the course of the later mediaeval centuries, from the late eleventh to the fifteenth century. It involved the acceptance by the secular power that it had no right to interfere in spiritual and sacramental tasks.

There was a tendency for religious motivations to transmute themselves into practical and secular ones. Some of those who migrated from Europe to America inspired by

Puritan ideals soon began to put their energies into getting control of lands and money and stock.[50] Yet at least a nostalgic sense of a higher purpose lingered. The Boston School Committee of 1853 still expressed a desire 'to take children at random from a great city, undisciplined, uninstructed, often with inherited stupidity of centuries of ignorant ancestors; forming them from animals into intellectual beings, and so far as a school can do it, from intellectual beings into spiritual beings'.[51]

Certain features of socially active grass-roots religious movements are notable in all these periods. They tended to be local, to place the emphasis on the group, with or without an obvious leader. They developed what theological expertise they could, with the help of sympathetic local clergy, if such help was to be had. Sometimes they contained highly educated individuals, or were fired by the example of a leading academic, but such influence was occasional rather than characteristic. With the exception of those on the extreme fringe, they tended to be hard-working, earnest, to be bourgeois from the centuries when the towns were developing. The 'Protestant work ethic', which held that God does not approve of idleness (cf. 2 Thessalonians 3.6–12) is to be found as early as Wyclif. He says that God 'abominates leisure in his rational creatures' (*abhominatur in creatura sua rationali ocium*).[52] The universal Church in its 'visible' form required organization on a scale which was beyond the control of small local groups. The traditional monastic orders were more or less closed except to the nobility. For 'ordinary people' to make their feelings felt, especially in the centuries where such people were ill-educated and unlikely to be able to achieve a great deal of 'social mobility', and when society did not allow entry to the nobility through talent or effort, was possible only if they formed their own groups and took charge of their own routes to seeking salvation. So that is what some of them did.

In a modern Western secular context the patterns have changed. The dissidents are no longer necessarily the under-privileged and the socially disadvantaged. But the liberation theology of Latin America saw active attempts by those who were not themselves among the outcasts, the poor, the help-less, to alter priorities in favour of those who are. The 'social Gospel' remains an imperative and proclaiming it still brings would-be followers of Christ's wishes into disrepute.

Christianity took social reform seriously only in comparat-ively modern times. William Wilberforce did something quite new when he tried to free the slaves of his day rather than encouraging them to obey their masters and hope for heaven. Perhaps the most striking modern counterpart of these medieval examples of social challenges which came to be condemned by heresy is the twentieth century movement, strongest in Latin America, known as liberation theology. The idea was to try to bring about in society a 'real-life' and 'this-worldly' version of the Christian promise of freedom and salvation. It makes a dramatic contrast with one of the most basic assumptions of the first Christian millennium, which was that to suffer in this world, to be poor or a slave or socially disadvantaged, was a help in getting to heaven.

Chapter 6

Good and Evil

Of all the mediaeval heresies, dualism challenged like no other the supremacy of the Christian God. Those who worship one God, who is omnipotent and wholly good, are left with the problem of evil. Again and again 'dualist' groups have arisen which have said that there must be some other power in the universe to account for evil, and have thus undermined the Christians' insistence that their God is omnipotent and wholly good. This thread runs consistently through the story of Christian heresy.

The earliest of the dualists, the Gnostics, existed before the birth of Christ, but they remained immensely influential in the earliest Christian period. Valentinus founded a second-century Gnostic sect known as the Valentinians. His popular dualist 'system' involved a crowd of personified numinous figures, easy for followers to 'grasp' or picture, for they played out a drama in heaven, good and evil at war. The Gnostics depicted this war in colourful and mythological terms, with the armies led by powers who were named characters in the battle. Marcion (d. c.160), though not perhaps strictly a Gnostic, was one of the leading figures in the second century to reject the Old Testament and its God, whom he, like many later dualists, depicted as a demiurge quite distinct from the God of Love revealed by Jesus. He thus encouraged the dualists of later ages to link this division of the Scriptures with the notion that there are two powers in the universe. Absolute dualists continued to rely on the New Testament. They took the Old Testament to be the work of the evil God, with the possible exception of portions of the Wisdom books and the prophets. The text from the apocryphal book of Ecclesiasticus, 'All things are double, one against another' (Ecclesiasticus 42.25), for example, was one the Cathars could warm to.

The Manichees, followers of the third century Persian dualist Mani, flourished in the time of Augustine. The Manicheans were sufficiently attractive to 'hold' Augustine for a decade as a follower of their teaching. Mani had regarded the human soul as a spark of the divine trapped in a material body. That and other dualist emphases upon the 'war within' each human being echoed Augustine's own personal experience as he struggled to 'subjugate the flesh', and even after he turned away from the Manichees and became a Christian, this sense of an inner duality never quite left him. Moreover, it chimed with the strong late antique emphasis on the virtues of asceticism, which embedded itself in the Christian tradition, and influenced many (such as Jerome) who did not go as far as to oppose flesh and spirit as the dualists did.

The Christian tradition, certainly by the time of Augustine in the West, had come to both a theological and a pastoral accommodation with all this. Augustine taught that evil is the absence of good, a 'nothing'. That is the only option open to orthodox Christian belief. If all that exists is God or made by God and God is wholly good, there appears to be no room for evil in the universe. Yet evil is manifestly powerful and damaging. Augustine's idea was that evil must be a turning away from God, the act of a rational creature with a will. And once the turning away has begun, there is nothing to hold back further deterioration, with all the consequences of an inability to think straight and a growing taste for the depraved and banal, to which Augustine points.

The weakness of the Augustinian explanation is that it does not explain 'cosmic' evil of the physical sort, such as an earthquake which kills thousands of 'innocent victims'. Augustine considers such happenings too to derive ultimately from the acts of will of rational creatures, but in any case he is confident that God can take them into his providential purpose, as he does all evil, and bring good from them.

The advantage of the Augustinian explanation is that it allows Satan to be real while maintaining that evil is nothing. He is a 'fallen angel', twisted in his thinking as a consequence of turning away from God. It was not unreasonable to ask how angels, with the unimaginable privilege of spending eternity in the presence of God, can possibly have turned away from bliss. In the late eleventh century Anselm of Canterbury says that the angels 'fell' because they aspired to be more like God than was appropriate to their creaturely natures. They longed for what was supremely good, but in a disorderly way. Thus was their pride their fall.

On this understanding, Satan is active, and full of evil intentions towards those who still love God. He tempted Adam and Eve and he lays siege to the souls of their descendants. Yet he is not another God, but a mere creature, the leader of the angels who fell at the beginning of the world, and however actively he works to tempt human beings away from God, he will in the end be overcome. This is the Antichrist of the Book of Revelation.

None of this is incompatible with a belief that a battle between good and evil is conducted within each human being. Although after 10 years Augustine became disillusioned with the Manichees he never quite shook off some of their ideas, and his continuing preoccupation with these had a lingering influence in the mediaeval West. They were ideas which had been pervasive in late antique philosophy, too, which made them influential in the Eastern half of the old Roman Empire, which did not on the whole read Augustine, as well as in the West. One of these important ideas was that spirit was good, and matter, if not the creation of the Evil God, as the dualists held, somehow less good and dangerous to spiritual aspiration. The body was material and it was subject to lusts which the human spirit found hard to control.

The Mediaeval Dualists

The shadow of the Manichees fell over Christian writing in the centuries after Augustine, partly because he wrote so much about them in later life, in an attempt to counter their teaching. Bede, for example, comments that 'the Manichee heretics are unsure about Christ and believe that he was not true flesh but spirit.'[1] Bede makes a list in which he distinguishes the pagans or 'gentiles' who worship 'many gods'; the (dualist) heretics who pollute the belief in one God with their errors; the Jews, who deny faith in Christ; the 'false catholics' who profane the right faith with wicked deeds of schisms.[2]

Some of the dualist literature in circulation in the Middle Ages was very ancient. The 'Vision of Isaiah', which may go back to the first century, describes in detail the ascent of the prophet Isaiah up through the realms of the heavens, where he saw for himself 'the great battle of Satan and his might opposing the loyal followers of God'. He asked the angel who was his guide, 'What is this war and envy and struggle'? The reply was, 'This is the Devil's war and he will not rest until he whom you wish to see comes to slay him with the spirit of his power.'[3]

It is important to distinguish the absolute from the moderate dualists. The views of the 'moderates' were not wholly irreconcileable with Christian orthodoxy. They did not insist on the existence of two gods; however, they regarded matter as evil. They said it was made in or through Satan, whom they regarded not as a god but as a creature. They saw this present world and human life in it as hell. Their idea was that the last judgement has already taken place, so the worst fate which can befall human beings is to remain as they are in this life.

The Paulicians, a seventh century Byzantine dualist sect, were precursors of mediaeval dualism. The Patriarch Nicephoros speaks of 'the evil and atheist throng' who were 'seeking a cult in which the icons and memorials of the Incarnation of Christ should not be seen'. In the Paulicians they found what they were looking for.[4] The Bogomils, Cathars and Albigensians were names used for dualist sects who posed a threat to Christian orthodoxy in the Middle Ages, especially in the late twelfth and early thirteenth centuries. Annals for the year 1041 contain a pun on the name of Mani ('maniac'). Those made insane by error took their name accordingly. They used to teach that the Father suffered with Christ and they made the sign of the cross on their foreheads with a single finger.

In the eleventh century, dualists were still visible in areas where the Eastern Church ruled or had an influence. The old Roman Empire had survived in part in the eastern Empire of Byzantium. About 1098, Anna Comnena, writer, caustic critic of the West, and member of the Imperial family, described the 'vast' numbers of heretics who had adopted a new and previously undiscovered form of heresy, that of the Bogomils. This, she said, combined the heresy of the Paulicians with that of the Messalians. The Messalians were a fourth century sect who concentrated on prayer. Their aim was to free themselves of the demons they believed to have entered into their souls and become pure spiritual beings for God. The Bogomil leader Basil was said to have 12 disciples. In defence of his teaching in the presence of the Emperor and his brother Isaac, Basil called the churches the temples of demons and mocked the Body and Blood of Christ. He was executed publicly in front of a large crowd, with his followers watching. A formula survives from the mid-twelfth century for use when a Bogomil was converted to Catholicisn. Those who had associated with the Bogomils but not worshipped with them nor taken part in their demonic nocturnal rites of initiation are to be received, instructed and should spend 40 days in prayer before forswearing their former errors. Those who have got further in, who have spent substantial time as members of the sect, are to spend twice 40 days in prayer and then to be handed over to a monastery, where they are to do penance in isolation for the rest of their lives.

Alan of Lille, in his late twelfth-century book against heretics, gives a summary of the dualist doctrine which he must have drawn chiefly from Augustine, but which also bears the marks of discussion in his own day:

> The heretics of our time say that there are two principles of things, the principle of light and the principle of darkness.

The principle of light, they say, is God, from whom are spiritual things, to wit, souls and angels. The principle of darkness, Lucifer, is he from whom are temporal things. . . . Since God is the highest good, evils are not from him; but since evils exist, and not from God himself, they come, therefore, from something other than God. Therefore, since God is the principle of good, there is another, the principle of evil. . . . At the beginning of Genesis, one reads that 'darkness was upon the face of the deep'. Thus the world had its beginning in darkness, and the founder of the world, who initiated its creator from darkness, was evil.[5]

The inquisitor Bernard Gui is a convenient starting-point for a catalogue of the views of the Manichees. His account exemplifies the difficulty which is to be encountered everywhere in the attempt to identify clear confessional positions held by those whose positions are condemned by the Church. Their views overlap. For example, he begins by explaining that they say there are two Gods (*duos deos asserunt*). They also say that there are two Churches, one good, one malign (*unam benignam, . . . aliam . . . malignam*), and that Rome is the Synagogue of Satan. But this is also Waldensian territory, for the 'modern Manichees' despise all the orders of the Church of Rome (*omnesque gradus et ordines ac ordinations eius despiciunt*). Then the modern Manichees are said to reject the sacraments and the resurrection of the body, which is in keeping with the dualist principle that matter is evil and the creation of the evil God. Yet rejection of the sacraments can also follow from rejection of the 'orders' of the Church.[6]

Rainerius, the former Cathar who became a Dominican, wrote a treatise in 1250 which includes detailed notes on respects in which Cathar 'substitutes' for the sacraments of the Church differ from those of orthodoxy. 'In true penance three things are requisite,' he explains, 'contrition of heart; confession of the lips; satisfaction by works'.

> But I, brother Rainerius, formerly a heresiarch but now by the grace of God a priest in the order of preachers, although unworthy, say positively and testify before God, who knows that I do not lie, that not one of these three appears among the Cathars or in their penance. For the poison of error which they have sucked from the mouth of the old serpent does not let them feel any sorrow for their sins. This error is fourfold, namely that eternal glory is not lessened for any penitent by any sin, that the punishment of hell is not increased thereby for the impenitent, that for no one is purgatorial fire reserved, and guilt and penalty are blotted out by God through the imposition of the hand. Judas the traitor will be punished no more severely than a child one day old.[7]

The *Book of Two Principles* is an anonymous dualist work of the thirteenth century. The author argues that it is logically necessary:

> to confess that there is another principle, one of evil, who works most wickedly against the true God and his creation; and this principle seems to move God against his own creation and the creation against its God, and causes God himself to wish for and desire that which in and of himself he could never wish for at all. Thus it is that through the compulsion of the evil enemy God yearns and is wearied, relents, is burdened, and is served by his own creatures.[8]

It emerges clearly in this text how strongly the dualists wanted to defend the goodness of a God who could, they argued, have no truck with evil. 'One should give no credence at all to the belief that the true Lord God absolutely and directly created darkness or evil, especially from nothing, which our opponents think is the proper meaning of "to create"'.[9]

In a thirteenth- or fourteenth-century Cathar gloss on the Lord's Prayer, 'deliver us from evil' prompts the comment that:

> the enemy, who has reigned over nations and over all men . . . is called not only Devil and Satan, but, in the interpretation of Holy Scriptures, he is also called the King of Assyria, who devoured the people and cut off their seat on high, and he seized the princes of the people, and placed his terror on earth among the living, and the cedars were not higher in the paradise of God.[10]

Mediaeval dualists carried forward the idea of the *perfecti*. The Manichees had had a system in which some of their members were regarded as *perfecti*. These were the elect, and other members mere adherents, who gained merit and helped the cause of the good by serving the 'Perfect'. The Cathars of the Middle Ages continued to call some of their members *perfecti*, in an age when the Christian emphasis was on a humble recognition of spiritual inadequacies and failings in the sight of God.[11] There was a reception ceremony, known as the *Consolamentum*, to admit a new member into the mediaeval Cathar community. It involved holding the Gospel over the candidate's head and invoking the Holy Spirit in Latin. The 'consoled' Cathars were then *perfecti*, and from that moment they were believed to be able to communicate with God, even though they continued to live in the hell of the present world. The new members were not made 'elect' by this ceremony. They were told that they must strive to 'live well' all their lives, while they continued to live in the evil world. These *perfecti* were believed, according to the records of the Inquisition, to be able to absolve everyone from their sins.[12]

The evidence from the Inquisition gives a clear indication of what the Church authorities believed mediaeval heresy to consist in, though of its nature it cannot be relied on to speak in the alleged heretics' own way. A list of Manichean heresies is preserved. It is said that they believe 'that there are two gods, one benevolent and the other malign; that the benevolent God made only spirit, and the malign god made all that bodily eyes can see. They say that this evil God is John the Baptist, whom they call the worst of the devils because Jesus said that the least in the kingdom of heaven was greater than him' (Matthew 11.11). They claim that Jesus's birth from Mary was spiritual not corporeal, that Jesus did not have real flesh and bones, did not eat or drink, did not die and was not resurrected because he was not truly a man or made of real flesh.[13]

The mediaeval Manichees are again depicted in this record as rejecting the sacraments, though for different reasons from those which led the Waldensians and their heirs to do so. The ordained ministry of the Church has no authority, say the Manichees, but only those of their own Church. So those who die in the Catholic Church go straight to hell, for their sins have not been forgiven; marriages contracted in the Catholic Church are not valid. Transubstantiation is of course denied, since there is no 'body' of Christ which the consecrated bread could become, and so the Eucharist is undermined.[14]

For the alleged Manichees interrogated, as for many of the subjects of the record of the Inquisition, there is a narrative of their actions, taken to be indicative of their false beliefs, followed by a summary of their errors.

Guilelmus Escaunerii speaks against blasphemy against the sign of the Cross, for the Manichees say that they ought not to make that sign or to show any reverence to the Cross, because the Lord was spat upon when he was crucified. He says that all who are received into his sect are immediately saved.[15]

Even witchcraft or Satanism is a dualist heresy, for its adherents worship the Devil in the confidence that he has powers which can counter those of God. Magic and witchcraft were natural associates of some of the more extreme heretical practices. A graphic example is given about 1182 by the English chronicler Walter Map. He relates how when the heretics are met,

> a black cat of marvellous size climbs down a rope which hangs in their midst. On seeing it they put out the lights. They do not sing hymns or repeat them distinctly, but hum through clenched teeth and pantingly feel their way towards the place where they saw their lord. When they have found him they kiss him, each the more humbly as he is the more inflamed with frenzy, some the feet, more the tail, most the private parts.[16]

The modern version of dualism is perhaps the kind of theology which challenges, as dualism classically did, the omnipotence or perfect goodness of God. The modern theologian who sees God as vulnerable or changeable is 'moving the goalposts' of the immutability which seemed to the earliest Christians to be one of his essential attributes.

Chapter 7

Dealing with Heresy

In most centuries the Church has been 'active' about heresy. As long as it was assumed that there was only one way to heaven, and that a narrow road, the Church's leaders could not rest while some of the flock were straying from that road and leading others to follow them.

The bishop's *cathedra*, or seat in the principal church of the diocese, gives the 'cathedral' its name. From that seat it was the duty of the bishop to preach. The homilies bishops delivered in the early Christian centuries principally involved exhorting their people to live holy lives and warning them when he thought their behaviour needed correction by explaining the Scriptures to them. But they also had a responsibility to make the faith clear to the people, and protect them from being led astray into unorthodox opinions. So both a 'positive' and a 'negative' theology (a theology 'in defence' of the faith), had a place.

The regularity, effectiveness and conscientiousness with which this all was done of course varied enormously. A preacher could be powerful, compelling or rather dull. From rare individuals such as an Augustine of Hippo or a Pope

Gregory I, we have surviving sermons of a quality which preserved them to be read in succeeding generations. Augustine could hold a congregation for two hours and win applause, and even without the impact of his oral delivery in person, his 'narrations' on the Psalms and his series of sermons on John's Gospel had enough in them to make them compelling reading for a thousand years.

There was, it seems, a lapse of any real expectation that bishops would regularly do this after about the time of Gregory the Great (c.540–604). His own sermons on Ezekiel are tense with the fears of a time when the barbarians were overrunning the remains of the Empire. But after him effort tended to go into monastic study and writing rather than into the preaching and preservation of new sermons by bishops maintaining and defending the faith. The 'bishop as baron' is a more characteristic figure of mediaeval Europe than the bishop as teacher.

The active revival of preaching skills in the twelfth and thirteenth centuries coincided chronologically with the rise of popular heresy – and who can say that it was not also a matter of cause and effect? But now it was not the bishops who were the preachers but the academics and certain leading monastic figures. Bernard of Clairvaux never went beyond the rank of abbot. In his influential series of 86 sermons on the Song of Songs, he interpreted the 'foxes' in a traditional way as 'heretics'. He explains in Sermon 64 that there are two kinds of 'fox', temptation and heresy. Heretical foxes are captured not with arms but with arguments to refute their errors. The aim is not to slay them but to recall them to the fold.[1] In Sermon 65 he is describing the 'new heretic' foxes of contemporary Cologne, who have been found shamelessly and unrepentantly cohabiting with women. In Sermon 66, he is discussing heretical foxes who condemn marriage and say that baptism is unnecessary and there is no benefit in praying for the dead.

Bernard's Order, the Cistercians, later became much involved with attempts to preach against a new manifestation of the dualism which had held Augustine captive for a decade, among the Albigensians or Cathars, chiefly in northern Spain and the south of France. At the beginning of the thirteenth century, this task was largely taken over by the order founded by St Dominic, which won papal approval in 1215. This was an order founded expressly to deal with heresy, and its members were trained especially to be persuasive preachers. They complemented the Franciscan Order, but their aim was different, in that they focused their efforts on the problem of heresy, whereas the Franciscans were (at first) simply trying to imitate Christ and preach the Gospel as he taught his disciples to do. The thirteenth-century rivalry between the two orders made them increasingly grow to resemble one another, but the Dominicans retained their first purpose and their preaching continued to concentrate mainly on the eradication of heresy and the conversion of heretics.

University Sermons

At the end of the twelfth century Alan of Lille created a manual of practical advice for preachers, including sets of ready-made materials for use in preaching on certain topics and to certain kinds of audience. This formal 'Art of Preaching' had successors from the 1230s in the form of other prescriptive manuals. An English example of the fourteenth century is that of Robert of Basevorn. His emphasis is on the living of the good Christian life. Preaching, he says, requires virtue in the preacher, a sufficient learning (especially in the Bible), and proper authority (*id est conscientia, scientia and potentia*). So he was clearly influenced by contemporary reservations about the break-away illicit preaching of dissidents. He particularly mentions women among those who may not preach.

The new preaching manuals were accompanied by various other aids, used by the friars in particular to help them in their preaching, such as collections of stock examples and stories, and dictionaries of biblical terms. The new type of sermon was mainly designed for academic audiences, and most of the sermons which survive are in Latin, even if they were at some stage preached in the vernacular for popular audiences.

The chief structural innovation made by these manuals was the habit of dividing the theme or 'text' of a sermon so as to treat it under subthemes and further subthemes. This kind of systematic approach is also reflected in the development of the *Summa*, or systematic treatment of theological topics in order. Aquinas's *Summa contra Gentiles* (or *Summa* against the unbelievers) includes in its first book disputes about the existence and being of God. Book II covers disputes about creation and particularly a topical and controversial question which was currently the subject of debate in the universities. The question was whether the world is eternal, as some ancient philosophers and Arab thinkers said, or whether it was created from nothing by God as Christians believed.[2] Book III deals with the problem of evil, which lies at the heart of dualism. Book IV is concerned with the errors which have arisen in the area of Christology.

Such a handbook would in principle enable those who found themselves meeting heretics and trying to convince them of the error of their ways to turn to the appropriate place and find exactly the contrary argument to use. Aquinas is not concerned to separate errors to be met in the streets of the cities of Europe in his own day from those of the remote past. He takes it, as did other apologists, that there is nothing very new in heresy; the same old ideas merely reappear in new guises.

The preaching of the 'professional preachers', the Mendicant orders, came in for criticism from dissidents and reformers. In his description of the proper motivation for preaching Wyclif criticizes the Mendicants for preaching only in order to get rich and to despoil their listeners. 'No one should preach in the name of Jesus except for the pure motive of saving souls'.[3] Christ's ascent to the mountain to preach teaches us that the preacher ought to 'teach the words of the Gospel' from on high downwards (*ab alto descendentia*), that is with a proper respect for their dignity. That means avoiding *apocrypha* and fables, and especially falsehood and greed. He does not believe the sects are really capable of understanding that.[4]

The Preaching of the Heretics Themselves

But the heretics were becoming noticeably interested in preaching too. One of the characteristic beliefs of the groups of popular heretics with 'anti-Establishment views' was that the ordained ministry should not have a monopoly of the right to preach, and especially of the right to interpret Scripture for the faithful. There was considerable anxiety about the consequence of letting self-appointed individuals preach, for if there was no control over the level of theological education required, and no requirement that they demonstrate their orthodoxy before they spoke, the faithful could very easily be led astray. We glanced at this problem in chapter 5, from the point of view of the social challenge of heresy

It raised with some sharpness the question of authority to preach. By the high Middle Ages the Church was extremely vigilant about this. It was a matter of having a licence from the bishop. Papal recognition of an 'order', such as those of the Franciscans and Dominicans whose very reason for existence was to preach the Gospel, could also confer authority to preach. In both cases the emphasis was upon ensuring that those who were allowed to lead others were themselves reliable in their orthodoxy.

This question grew more pointed still with the coming of the pre-Reformation period and the Reformation itself, for it merged into another question we met in an earlier chapter. Preaching as a means of addressing the problem of heresy took on an altered complexion in the Reformation period. The reformers greatly emphasized the importance of the Ministry of the Word. They took that to mean not only giving Scripture its proper place, but also 'teaching' the Bible by expounding it.

Could individual Christians safely be allowed to read the Bible for themselves in their own language? Or must they depend on the preaching of a professional clergy who had privileged access to it in Latin and the theological education to understand it?

Popular calls for freedom to preach and freedom to read the Bible in the vernacular became topical together, and it was for similar reasons that the Church reacted at first with hostility to both. There was a legitimate fear that the faithful would go astray if left to themselves in this way. It was generally assumed in the mediaeval Church that the simple faithful could not be trusted to stay within the theological boundaries of orthodoxy because they were ignorant. It was even sometimes suggested that less was required of them because of their very simplicity, although that little must be strictly orthodox. By the sixteenth century, in reforming communities, the emphasis had shifted to providing the Bible in the vernacular and letting the laity have it. Royal wishes could be confused and contradictory, and there was wrangling about the approval of particular translations. But Henry VIII of England issued a proclamation in 1541 that all parishes 'Not having already Bibles provided within their churches, shall . . . buy and provide Bibles of the largest and greatest volume' in English, and these were to be made available to parishioners so that they could 'learn thereby to observe God's commandments, and to obey their sovereign Lord'.

The solution of ensuring that the ordinary faithful did not remain ignorant by giving them a proper theological education was not explored with any enthusiasm by the mediaeval Church's authorities. Even the clergy were often not well educated theologically. They went no further than the provision of formal catechisms with standard answers.

The attempt to educate at least the young faithful was to await the initiatives of individuals, and it was not to begin until much later. Robert Raikes (1735–1811), for example, encountered considerable opposition when he sought to establish Sunday Schools to teach children to read and some basic theology and knowedge of the Bible, because it was still feared, even in late eighteenth- and nineteenth-century England, that to teach the ignorant populace was to incite them to revolution.

Persuasion by preaching, then, had mixed success. If heretics cannot be persuaded can they be compelled? The most notable example of 'crusading against heretics' is the Albigensian Crusade which was instigated by Pope Innocent III after the assassination of his legate. In 1207 he had written to the French King and to a number of French noblemen encouraging them to use military force to suppress heretics in their territories. They were promised that they would be able to keep any property captured in this way and that they would enjoy the indulgence which had been given to the crusaders who went to the Holy Land. At first they were not enthusiastic, for the local nobility had Cathars among them, and the papal legate sent to stir them to action was assassinated in 1208 by a knight who was in the service of the Count of Toulouse. Angry, the Pope added to the incentives he was offering. He promised release from the payment of interest on debts to those who joined his crusade against the Albigensian heretics. He exempted them from the jurisdiction of the secular courts. So long as they served for at least 40 days, he offered absolution from all sins.

Simon de Montfort led the actual fighting in this 'crusade', which was, in the end, largely the work of northern French nobles; it lasted for two decades. It was notable for its brutality and its tendency to merge and transform itself into the familiar territorial battles of mediaeval Europe. In 1209 the city of Béziers was sacked and pillaged. In answer to the question how the 'crusaders' were to know which of the townspeople were heretics the Papal Legate is said to have ordered that they should be killed indiscriminately, for God would know his own. A decade of brutality and excess followed, until Simon de Montfort himself was killed in 1218. There were fresh waves of 'crusading' effort, but the momentum was gradually lost and Cathar resistance had died away by the mid-1250s.

There were limits to what a crusade might achieve. It might bring back 'territory' to the nominal control of the Church, of the control of nobles loyal to the Church, but it still did not necessarily bring individuals into the fold. There was a debate in the fourteenth century about whether it could ever be justified to kill infidels.

The Church's task was to save souls. In notes for lecturing or preaching, Robert Holcot (d.1349) assembled the standard arguments for and against the ultimate execution of those who obstinately refused to be won back to the faith. Dead infidels could never repent and the work of grace in them was cut off at their death. The important question being tested in this discussion was whether there was any salvation outside the Church. For if God could save even heretics by the secret operation of his grace, it could not be right to put them to death.[5]

Nevertheless, executing heretics by burning them at the stake remained the ultimate sanction against them. It could be justified as giving them a last chance to recant, for a heretic who was converted back to orthodoxy at the moment of death could hope for heaven. It was therefore in theory not mere punishment, but something which could be said to be for the burning heretic's ultimate good.

Inquisition

Inquisition is, on the face of it, a less extreme method of dealing with heresy and heretics than crusade. But it was

Plate 7   William Tyndale being burnt at the stake, woodcut from Foxes's *Acts and Monuments of Martyrs*, 1684. Private collection.

Plate 8   Galileo before the Inquisition, Rome, 1633, painting by J. N. R. Fleury. Musée du Louvre, Paris/photo AKG London, Erich Lessing.

not systematically tried until after the Albigensian Crusade when, in 1233, Pope Gregory IX instituted the Inquisition. This coincided quite closely with moves in the legal world to abbreviate the procedures for trial, and to proceed on the basis of information laid by informers.

'The special jurisdiction exercised by delegates of the Pope for the repression of heresy', or 'the Inquisition' began in 1231, after the ending of the Albigensian Crusade in 1229 with the Treaty of Meaux-Paris. It had been authorized in principle by the second decree of the Fourth Lateran Council of 1215. That decree excommunicated and anathematized heretics of every kind and required each bishop 'either in person or through his archdeacon or other suitable honest persons' to visit each parish once or twice a year. 'There he should compel three or more men of good repute, or even if it seems expedient the whole neighbourhood', to point out on oath any in the parish who 'hold secret conventicles' (*conventicula*) or 'who differ in their life and habits from the normal way of living' (*a communi conversatione fidelium vita et moribus dissidentes*).

The bishop is to summon those thus accused and if they are unable to clear themselves of the charge, or if after they have recanted on oath they relapse into their former errors, they are to be subject to canonical punishment. Those who refuse to swear to their orthodoxy of faith will by virtue of their very refusal to take an oath be deemed heretics (*ex hoc ipso tamquam heretici reputentur*).[6] The bishop himself is to be put under considerable pressure, for he is to be deposed if he fails to perform these duties conscientiously and rigorously.

The business of refusal to take the oath was important, and it features in a prominent position in the records of the Inquisition, since for some dissidents, particularly the Waldensians, it was a matter of principle in itself even though at every other point they might be prepared to conform.

The refusal to take an oath was taken by the Inquisition to be a safe 'marker' of the presence of heretical leanings. Bonacursus says that the Cathars believe that everyone who swears an oath will be damned.[7] It was a reluctance widespread among many types of heretic and rested on the scriptural principle of Matthew 5.37 ('Let your speech be "yes, yes" and "no, no"'). Behind stood Psalm 76.11, with its instruction to make vows to God (only?) and to keep them.[8] In the case of Ramundus Valeira, the bishop conducting the inquisition received from Ramundus a *corporale iuramentum*, that is an oath taken on the Gospel, which was actually touched.[9]

One effect of the decree was to bring the same individuals back before the Inquisition every year, as the record shows, for once under suspicion a 'heretic' could be regarded as always liable to backsliding. Moreover, it could be difficult to persuade suspicious inquisitors of the genuineness of any recantation. One Guillelmus Autastz failed to do so and it is recorded that 'on the information laid, it was evident that the said Guillelmus was not telling the truth'; he was sent to prison.[10] Once on the list for recall, a 'heretic' was likely to produce other names for inquiry. A key question technique of the Inquisition was to ask heretics who were being questioned whether they knew of other heretics. They are asked who they know; where they are to be found and whether they have been mixing with them. When did this begin? Have they ceased to mix with them? The drift of such questioning made it difficult for the alleged heretics to emerge free from blame themselves.[11]

There are surviving records of the detailed conduct of Inquisitions. The *Register* of Jacques Fournier during his time as Bishop of Pamiers from 1317 preserves a series of interrogations of individuals brought back year after year for further questioning.[12] This is one of the consequences of the requirements of 1215, which had apparently not been eased by the new rules of reasonableness and moderation under the Council of Vienne. Interrogation of women might be briefer than that of men but Agnes, wife of Stephen Francus, for example, was tested with the question whether she would take an oath, and women could be asked if they were acquainted with other 'known' heretics. Agnes was asked whether she knew Raymundus de Costa.[13] The attempt to get individuals to inform on one another was still vigorously pursued a century after Lateran IV. Berengarius is asked whether he knows both Raymond and Agnes.[14]

The Jews could be the target of such investigations as well as Christian heretics. They were forced into conversions for political and economic reasons, as well as out of a strictly religious motivation.

So we have, in effect, two pictures of the Inquisition, the one which tells us how it ought to be conducted and the one which hints at what really happened. We lack an equivalent detailed perspective from the point of view of the repeatedly accused individuals. The *Manuel de l'Inquisiteur* of Bernard Gui is an instruction manual of the early fourteenth century when the system had been running for a century.[15] Gui intended his handbook to meet the needs of those dealing with heretics in the Narbonne region of France in the aftermath of the Council of Vienne of 1311–12, which had recognized that the conduct of the Inquisition could be oppressive and that it was losing sight of the principles on which it was set up. It had been intended to root out heresy, but was becoming an instrument of tyranny over ordinary people, many of whom had no idea that they could be labelled unorthodox in their faith.

That Council promulgated among its 'constitutions' one known as *Multorum querela*[16] and another called *Nolentes*.[17] The first, whose opening words are *'Multorum querela'*, concerns the complaints received by the Holy See that some inquisitors have overstepped the limits of the power given to them. Sometimes by their conduct they transform a provision which was wisely designed by the Holy See for the promotion of the faith into an instrument of oppression of the innocent. It is insisted that the work must be done with discretion and without an eye to self-interest. It must be done by bishop and inquisitor together, with no harsh sentences imposed by either sitting alone. 'While it is a grave offence not to work for the extermination of heresy . . . it is also a grave offence . . . maliciously to impute such wickedness to the innocent'. *Nolentes* adds an insistence that only persons of mature age (over 40) should allowed to be inquisitors, and makes an attempt to ensure that there is no extortion and bribery in the conduct of the process.

Bernard Gui's manual provides guidance, some of it relating to earlier periods of Inquisition, some of it reflecting these new rules, a formulary for notaries of the episcopal Inquisition, a collection of sentences of the Inquisition of Toulouse from 1308–23, and some borrowings from the earlier writings of others.[18]

Bernard is conscious of the need for those dealing with heretics to be informed about the reasons (*rationes*) and authorities (*auctoritates*) by which they are accustomed to support themselves in argument. The simple laity are easily misled by those who present themselves as experts and then become stumbling-blocks for the faithful. The heretics are cunning in this respect.[19] It is easy to mislead thereby verbal fallacies (*quia per fallacies verborum et per excogitates astutias dilabuntur*). It is the more important to have 'sure and sufficient testimonies against them' (*certa et sufficientia testimonia contra ipsos*).

It is not easy to say what it meant when a heretic 'confessed'. The bishop acting as inquisitor is seeking a confession from the heretic, under pain of punishment, and where things would be by no means 'over', for the confessed heretic would be re-examined on the Inquisition's next visit. The priest as confessor is also seeking a confession, but within the penitential process, where the purpose is one of healing and reconciliation. One of the dissident behaviours frequently disapproved of was the practice among the anti-Establishment groups of the later Middle Ages of claiming that anyone could hear his or her brother's or sister's confession. This threatened the ordained ministry at one of its most important points, for the authority to grant absolution was reserved to the priesthood. This was the power of the keys, the power to bind and loose in heaven and hell, which Christ had entrusted to his disciples (Matthew 16.19). The dissidents could quote James (5.16) where it seemed that all Christians were free to do this for one another, but the Church was determined to insist that the priesthood alone had the necessary authority.

The Change in the Balance of Power

Polemic expresses anger. It is also the vehicle of adversaries, formerly an oppressed class of the condemned, who were beginning to feel their strength in a new world order. Wyclif's exegesis on the subject of popular access to the Bible is full of polemic. Preaching *ad populum* on Matthew 21.1 (*Iesus misit duos discipulos*), Wyclif explains that the two disciples are *presybteri et seculars*, priests and seculars, and that it is their duty to speak out against the *castellani*, the keepers of the *castellum* which appears later in this passage. The *castellani* are the beneficed clergy who are, says Wyclif 'always' against the disciples of Christ (*semper contra Christi discipulos*).[20] It is possible to identify 'sideswipes' at his enemies again and again. In his third sermon on the Sunday Gospels he mentions John the Baptist's notable unconcern for soft raiment (*mollia vestimenta*) and he does not resist adding 'unlike the Friars!'[21] Addressing the question of the definition of 'prophet' he remarks in passing on the unhelpful definition of 'many in the sects'.[22] Again, 'the disciples of Antichrist' falsely say that the construction of rich buildings (churches) is 'necessary to the Christian religion', basing their argument on the fallacy that since God cannot have too splendid a house, it is incumbent on the laity to build him the best they can so as to honour him.[23] In his *On the Foundation of the Sect* (V-XV) he gives biblical proofs for his assertions that the *sects* were not only superfluous but also harmful, and others. The 16th chapter takes him to methodological questions of exegesis, but again with an irritability on the subject of the 'sects' which frequently gets in the ways of his reflection on Scripture.[24]

The 'biblical ecclesiology' Wyclif expounds on Matthew 5–7 and 23–5 and John 13–17 bears all the characteristic marks of polemic, in its repeated sideswipes at his enemies. For example, in I.vi he gives Robert Grosseteste's list of the signs of humility. He points out that the Pope lacks them all, and that enables him to move on to the theme of the Pope as usurper.[25] This he readily couples with the accusation that the Curia neglects the study of Scripture. Those working at the Curia, he says elsewhere,[26] can see for themselves that they are in the abomination of desolation and hear blasphemy and lies, but they do not respond by setting out the senses of Scripture and nothing they say is directed to the salvation of the soul.

Wyclif and his generation were still doing something dangerous when they shouted at the authorities. But all that was to change in the sixteenth century, when the adversaries became much more equal, and we move to the defiant writings of a Luther and the establishment of rival Churches.

Living with Difference

There is another way of 'dealing with heresy' and that is to regard it as legitimate difference and live with it. A willingness to 'live with difference', unthinkable in the first Christian centuries, could and did have a number of causes. In the sixteenth century West it was sometimes recognized that there are a number of matters on which the Church need not insist, indeed, on which it has not really made up its mind. There was no compromise of the fundamentals involved here, because such points were taken to be not fundamental.

There is a natural philosophical and historical bridge between the idea that some beliefs are fundamental or essential and others indifferent, and the development of toleration. Toleration is appropriate only when there are strong and polarized views and yet society no longer accepts that one faction or opinion is entitled to exclude or punish the other. That was the case for a century or two after the end of the Middle Ages, but it has been unusual historically for toleration to be approved of. Until well after the sixteenth century, the consistent assumption of every century was that religious beliefs were either 'right' or 'wrong', that conflicting views, at least on key points of faith, could not both be accommodated. To think otherwise was to risk the souls of those who were in error and the spiritual safety of others whom they might lead astray. 'Perhaps toleration will prove to have been an interim value, serving a period between a past when no one had heard of it and a future in which no one will need it', suggests Bernard Williams.[27]

Toleration is largely a creation of the seventeenth century, although there is a remarkable early tract by Sebastian Castellio written in 1554. Castellio was a Calvinist who had already begun to part company with Calvin on the subject of the need to accept a broad range of views. He was shocked by Calvin's execution of Severus, and wrote *On Heretics* as a call for toleration of those who differed in belief. In the background to the fuller development of an ideal of toleration lie the polemical exchanges of the sixteenth and seventeenth centuries, in which points in dispute could be tossed backwards and forwards in pamphlets, to the accompaniment of a good deal of personal abuse, with potentially unedifying and confusing effects on the faithful.

In 1630 the Jesuit Edward Knott (whose real name was Matthias Wilson) published *Charity Mistaken*, in which he maintained that 'Protestancy unrepented destroys salvation'. There followed a long exchange during which *Charity Mistaken* prompted *Charity Maintained*, and the seventeenth-century English polemicist William Chillingworth became involved, along with others, with the Archbishop of Canterbury, William Laud, eventually being obliged to look into what was going on. Chillingworth was prepared to 'grant, that Christ founded a visible church, stored with all helps necessary to salvation, particularly with sufficient means to beget and conserve faith, to maintain unity and compose schisms, to discover and condemn heresies, and to determine all controversies in religion which were necessary to be determined'. But he says that it cannot be essential that all controversies are determined immediately by these means. Manifestly some controversies go on for many ages, and 'meanwhile men be saved'. If it is really 'necessary that all controversies in religion should be determined', why is 'the question of predetermination, of the immaculate conception, of the pope's indirect power in temporalities, so long undetermined?'[28] His idea was that Protestants are not heretics, because 'it is not heresy to oppose any truth propounded by the Church, but only such a truth as is an essential part of the Gospel of Christ'.[29]

The poet and controversialist John Milton in his *Areopagitica*, and some among the contemporary Baptists, Congregationalists and Quakers, strove to get it accepted that it could be God's will that Christians should show one another toleration. Controversy spreads the infection of heresy, Milton thinks, and he was in part moved by a consciousness that religious controversy can spread the 'infection' of novel and erroneous ideas. This is 'most and soonest catching to the learned, from whom to the common people what ever is hereticall and dissolute may quickly be conveyed'.[30] However, Milton excluded the Roman Catholics from this call to mutual charity,

The political philosopher John Locke (1632–1704), wrote a series of *Letters Concerning Toleration* (1689, 1690, 1692), calling for toleration for believers of all complexions, again with the exception of those who were Roman Catholics or atheists. His reason for excluding these was that he considered them a danger to the state, in the particular circumstances of a post-Reformation Protestant England in which the Church of England was 'established' and stood in an intimate relationship with the state. Atheists were unreliable because they could not be expected to respect the sanctity of an oath taken on the Bible. 'Those are not at all to be tolerated who deny the being of God' because 'promises, covenants and oaths, which are the bind of human society, can have no hold upon an atheist'.[31]

Locke's Latin *Epistola de Tolerantia* was published anonymously in 1689 and a translation by William Popple came out in the same year. Popple wanted to encourage Locke's readers to see the issues largely. 'Our Government,' he said in his 'To the Reader', 'has not only been partial in matters of religion, but those who have suffered under that partiality and have therefore endeavoured by their writings to vindicate their own rights and liberties, have for the most part done it upon narrow principles. Suited only to the interests of their own sects'.[32]

Locke himself offers a new ecclesiology, a theology of the Church which turned on its head some of the central presumptions of the past. 'The mutual toleration of Christians in their different professions of religion . . . I esteem . . . to be the chief characteristical mark of the true church'.[33] Locke's definition of a church begins from the individual conscience and emphasizes the 'gathering for worship' which was the preferred way of a number of protestant ecclesial communities: 'A church then I take to be a voluntary society of men, joining themselves together of their own accord, in order to the public worshipping of God, in such a manner as they judge acceptable to him, and effectual to the saving of their souls'.[34]

He observes, in a striking departure from the assumption of the primitive Church, that 'everyone is orthodox to himself' and identifies the striving of those holding one set of opinions for mastery over those holding another as 'much rather marks of men's striving for power and empire over one another, than [marks] of the church of Christ.'[35] It follows that even where someone has to be cast out of the community because of his or her behaviour, the excommunication should be carried out gently. And in Locke's view, 'No private person has any right in any manner to prejudice another person in his civil enjoyments because he is of another Church or religion'.[36] Nor has any Church 'any manner of jurisdiction over any other', even if it has the approval of the civil magistrate, 'for the civil government can give no new right to the church, nor the church to the civil government'.[37] That would be true even if it could be certain which was 'right'.[38]

The danger and damage is much more than a mere misplacement of priorities. There is danger to souls in 'the divisions that are among sects'; it is 'obstructive to salvation'.[39] More, it is likely to tempt the state to think that it can save souls by secular force.[40]

Locke lays down another important principle. Someone who is not a Christian at all cannot be a schismatic or a heretic. What would now be called 'inter-faith dialogue' falls outside the boundaries of the discussion.[41]

There can be a decline in the sheer level of active concern about religion in the population. In a modern world, large parts of which are now decidedly secular, there can be an 'undeclared state of heresy' when people may be unclear and inarticulate about their own beliefs. Many may not understand clearly what is orthodox and what is not, when it does not seem to them very important.[42]

Alongside such dropping away of mass consciousness of religious issues may go a heightening of political resistance or civil disobedience. Burning the flag, or refusing to join in or to stand up respectfully when the national anthem is played, may seem in the modern world as much a 'social heresy' as refusal to worship the Emperor was in the ancient world. The state may treat these as a challenge to symbols of society which have an almost 'religious' significance. Yet it is not always the case in the modern world that civil disobedience or even participation in 'wars of religion' is motivated by the willingness to die for one's faith. It can be primarily or largely political in its motivation. It may also be extremely confused. When it is possible to take a long view of the reaction of the United States of America to the bombing of the 'twin towers' in New York on 11 September 2001, it may be possible to trace in that exactly this kind of confusion or collation of political with religious reasons for conflict. The 'terrorist enemy' was readily 'identified' in certain Islamic states, although there was no testing of the evidence in court, and America and her 'allies' went to war in Afghanistan. Dissent from and objection to this course of action, particularly by academics, in the USA was frowned on and put down quite repressively. To criticize the 'war against terrorism' as a 'war of religion' was deemed 'un-American'.

To think in terms of 'dealing with heresy' at all is now becoming an anachronism. In the West the modern way would be to try to meet 'heretics' as fellow believers where they are and and seek a way of stating shared belief; or to allow them space to be themselves. But elsewhere in the world – and indeed in the West itself, if we include such areas as Northern Ireland and Bosnia – ancient tribal division still manifest themselves as religious wars. There is a considerable distance between 'progressive' theory and the still-brutal practicalities. Nowhere is that more apparent than in the rationalization of the 'war on terrorism' which began in September 2001.

Conclusion

Let us go back to where we began, and the 'first principles'. Throughout the New Testament appear 'reminders' of the importance of those principles to the first Christians. Luke 14.15–24 describes the 'banquet' to which people were to be brought in from the town alleys and country lanes to fill the house of God. Once within the Church Christians are to be one body in one Spirit, the Holy Spirit (Ephesians 4.3–4). Galatians 1.6–9 condemns anyone who adheres to a different version of the Gospel. Such newcomers (innovators?) are described as cunning as serpents (2 Corinthians 11.3). 1 Timothy 6.4–5 describes the sowing of jealousy, contention, abuse and mutual mistrust among the faithful. Hebrews is fierce about the way such individuals should be treated if they are denounced by two or three witnesses (Hebrews 6.8, 10.26–31).

The apparent simplicity of these directives led to the intolerance which has been visible in these pages. It encouraged rigidity, the playing of power-games, oppression, and – when the heretics were articulate enough to answer back – adversariality and polemic. These are hard to reconcile with the message of a Christ who came to bring peace. Yet the same Christ threw the money-changers out of the Temple and warned that he had come to set members of families against one another. The story of the process which led to his crucifixion makes it plain that his message was regarded as countercultural by the authorities of his day.

Part of the problem has been that the Church did not always know what else to do other than 'crack down'. The Humiliati, for example, moved from one side to the other of the borderline of respectability for some time, until, in the early thirteenth century, Pope Innocent III wrote to ask them to state their position.[1] But the fate of those who called others to 'imitate Christ' and 'live the apostolic life' has, in the end, usually been official condemnation. The 'official Church', once it became wealthy and powerful and stood in a compromising relationship with the state, had much to lose by any other course of action. It could not control these 'simple followers'. They had a missionary bent; the Anabaptists' missionary movements of the late eighteenth and nineteenth centuries, for example, speak of Christ's Great Commission. That meant they multiplied. They flourished on persecution, seeing it as persecution for the sake of righteousness. About 1214 one Yves of Narbonne, who had been accused of heresy before Robert of Courson, Papal Legate, was forced to become a wanderer. When he found himself among the Cathar sympathizer 'Patarines' in Como in Italy he says 'they were pleased to hear this and considered me fortunate to be persecuted for the sake of righteousness'. He dwelt among them for three months, enjoying their lavish hospitality, and held his tongue as he heard daily 'the many errors, or rather horrors, which they propounded against the apostolic faith'.[2]

Against such, remorselessness may be ineffective, but the authorities have usually seen no other way.

The marks of the Church which were insisted on in the early Christian centuries (that it is one, holy, catholic and apostolic) are the marks of a body of Christ whose unity was of its essence. Yet within the Church that unity was under strain from a very early stage as power struggles emerged. When the Church condemned heretics and dissidents it was not only seeking to preserve the integrity and purity of the faith; it was also defending the monolith of an increasingly centralized ecclesial authority. One lesson of a brief history of heresy therefore may be that being persecuted may not be a direct consequence of posing a threat to the true faith and right order, but primarily of being a nuisance to powerful figures and interest groups. This may make such individual dissidents more 'political' than 'religious', and cloud the notion of being 'persecuted for righteousness' sake'. It can be illuminating to trace this kind of thing backwards from the modern world where political dissidence is a familiar phenomenon, to earlier periods where the political coloration of religious dissidence is less obvious.

Noam Chomsky 'came out more and more strongly against the apparently willing collaboration of the intellectual community with the state' in late twentieth-century USA.[3] He was critical of 'media collusion with powerful elites' and of 'collusion between intellectuals and state policies, even when these policies are clearly oppressive, violent or illegal'.[4] He found himself the subject of reviews questioning the 'status' of his linguistic work, and there was 'an effort to find fault with Chomsky's work in the form of factual errors. But, aside from some trivial slips, Chomsky stood up to the test'.[5]

'It is only in Christian countries that free speech is known at all,' commented the late nineteenth-century journalist Ambrose Bierce.[6] He did not like to see that freedom undermined by a 'politicized' Church leadership. At the turn of the twentieth century, he was writing, as a journalist, to lament the conflict between the positions taken by leaders of the Church who were the powerful elite of their day, and the fundamentals of Christ's teaching, the call to a life of poverty and simplicity. His particular criticism of the Church is over its support for war: 'The "unbeliever" has a logical right to regard war as refining and ennobling if he can, and to say so if he does, but no professed Christian can hold such a belief and utter it without forfeiting the respect of all who know and love the character of Jesus Christ'. But his point is really wider. He attacks the 'fat patriot and smooth hierarch', the Bishop of Armagh, who 'dates his poem at his "palace" – this disciple of the Prince of poverty who had not where to lay his head! And this is Christianity – this corrupted cult within whose wide confines a luxurious clergy . . .' and so on.[7]

As we go back further still we find the heretic as whistle-blower appearing as a familiar figure again and again. Jan Hus's bewilderment echoes down the centuries. 'Very often I repeat to myself that not long ago after your enthronement Your Paternity had set up the rule that whenever I should observe some defect in the administration, that I should instantly report such defect.'[8] Straightforward obedience of this sort was, it turned out, not only not 'received' in a constructive spirit; it brought down retribution on his head, so that he was prompted to complain:

> This rule now compels me to express myself: how is it that
> fornicating and otherwise criminal priests walk about freely

and without rigorous correction . . . while humble priests . . . who fulfil the duties of your administration with proper devotion, are not avaricious, but offer themselves freely for God's sake to the labour of proclaiming the Gospel – these are jailed as heretics and suffer exile for the very proclamation of the Gospel? . . . What poor priests will dare to fight against criminal conduct? Who will dare to make known vices?[9]

These tendencies are illustrated by the events of the trial of Jan Hus at the Council of Constance. This Council had urgent political purposes of considerable importance for the future of the Church. There had been an unusually long-drawn-out dispute as to who was the authentic pope, and the opportunity was taken to try to settle the matters at issue in the resulting Great Schism, and also to achieve a balance between the powers of the bishops and the by now monarchical authority of the papacy. The Council was, in the end, a failure, and it left unresolved the serious problems of papal plenitude of power, the role of councils and the role of the laity. This failure was a major factor in the process which then led onwards to the Reformation.

It has been suggested more than once in these pages that the sixteenth century in the West saw a development which had no precedent in Christian history. Dissidents became 'reformers' and a series of alternative 'Churches' came into being side by side and have continued in existence, still side by side and unreconciled, since the Reformation. Not all the members of such communities have recognized the others as truly ecclesial. Indeed, the whole question 'what is the Church?', which has been hovering in every page of this book, was thrown into new uncertainty by the new scene.

The Roman Catholic Church in particular still would not countenance the existence of these 'others' at the time when the World Council of Churches was established, and would not 'join' a World Council of Churches. The Second Vatican Council of the 1960s expressed itself in language still resistant to the full acceptance that there could be other bodies, not in communion with the See of Rome, which were 'truly the Church'.

Equally, many reformers in and since the Reformation have shared a belief that the single universal historic 'visible' Church, with the Pope at its head, was no longer the Church at all, because it had strayed from the way Christ had intended it to follow when he told Peter that he was the rock on which he intended to build his Church. A leading idea of the period among reformers was that the Church is invisible, a community of grace, a mystical community, which can be 'seen' only in the small local worshipping community. For some reformers, the emphasis now fell on those small 'gathered' communities. The idea was that the Church was to be 'found' worshipping in each place. (A modern manifestation of this kind of thinking is the 'house church'.) The local churches were thus visible small parts of the great invisible Church. This was a quite different idea from the 'Church-in-each-place' of the orthodox, for whom the local Church is a microcosm of the Church, in such a way that the whole Church is present in each place. For other sixteenth-century reformers, the Church is a communion of saints which transcends space and time, but they were content to retain all or most of the structures of the visible Church, an ordained ministry and a formal order and liturgy.

Once we arrive at the Reformation there is radical change, not of the assumption of each group in the new divisions that it is the true Church and is uniquely preserving the unity of the faith and a right order in the Church, but of the possibility that they can all be right. Heresy has become division. The balance has changed. There is no longer a powerful dominant ecclesial body calling a small number of miscreants to order but the marshalling of sometimes numerically or politically equal 'forces'. Erastianism, with its notion that each locality should have its own religion, was in keeping with the belief of many protestant leaders that the local 'magistrate' or secular authority was a proper figure to lend its authority to the local Church.

The invention of printing and the rise of protagonists well-matched in theological knowledge and eloquence, fostered a polemical literature. The sixteenth and seventeenth century abounds in pamphlet warfare, as we saw in the example of William Chillingworth.

'Conversion' can mean a real change of view, a *metanoia*, not only bringing individuals to the faith but also sometimes changing their position as Christians. Chillingworth and Newman both experienced moments of that sort. That is the first stirring of an attitude to Christian difference out of which it was ultimately possible for modern ecumenism to grow.

An inter-faith dialogue of the modern kind has become possible only as the idea of 'mission' has been transformed. Missionary movements of the nineteenth and early twentieth century went out from Europe to what is now known as the 'Third World', patronizingly taking with them the assumption that they were bringing not only Christianity but civilization. Their objective was to convert people 'from' the religion in which they found them and 'to' Christianity. The 'other' religion was regarded as inferior and dangerous to souls in that it was not able to bring people to salvation. The great change of the late twentieth century was towards a dialogue between faiths which met each other as equals.

Inter-faith dialogue is a field more fraught even than that of Christian ecumenism, since ecumenism can presume on a fundamental unity which needs only to be rediscovered or recaptured. Inter-faith dialogue cannot lead to agreement in a single faith. That is not its objective. Yet it can encourage Christians engaged in it into a form of Arianism as they try to accept that perhaps Christ is not the only Messiah, the sole Saviour of humankind.

In the twentieth century it began to be acceptable to recognize the need for a degree of 'accommodation' in modern Christianity in parts of the world where the local culture did not sit easily with Christian expectations. In some African societies, as we noticed earlier, polygamy was the norm and Christians in such places were faced directly with a decision whether to insist on monogamy. The resulting 'inculturation' could itself be divisive, if the world Church could not accept that polygamy could be compatible with Christianity, but is has also been an instrument of change and enlargement of the primitive Christian idea of the incompatibility of unity and diversity.

The reality is that at the beginning of the third millennium Christianity and its struggle with its own identity are hard to detach from the social and secular environment. There is no longer a widespread respect for a body of authoritative tradition against which disputes can readily be tested. Too much is in the melting-pot. Too much freedom of choice for the individual, at least in Western societies, makes people unwilling to bend to rulings. They argue. They think for themselves, sometimes with insufficient evidence. They take positions, sometimes without the training to use language exactly or the knowledge to see that the position is in fact a classic heresy. The 'American Way of Life' could be called Pelagianism, for it teaches that people can both be good and 'get on in life' simply by trying hard. Self-improvement manuals are in the same tradition. Feminist insistence on revision of 'paternalist' language in speaking of the Trinity can easily lead into some of the classic Trinitarian heresies in which the Persons of the Trinity were given separate attributes. To call the Father 'Creator' instead is to do exactly that. The fringe religions inspired by vague notions of Far Eastern spirituality, the neo-witchcraft, the séances, the popular horoscopes, the promises of the sects, are very commonly dualist in inspiration.

Heresy has been a great shaker-up of complacency. There are those who react against authority, and may become persistent and vociferous and trouble the authorities, but in the end make a difference. For there has been a change of attitude in the way the Church approaches the question of heresy. The modern ecumenical movement is inclusive, not exclusive. Since the creation of the World Council of Churches from the beginning of the twentieth century, and particularly since the Second Vatican Council, the unity of the Church has become an objective which does not assume that it can be possible or is right to try to return to uniformity. The united Church of the future will be more generous, richer and possessed of a set of priorities which distinguish the core issues of faith and order from matters where there can properly be some room for individual and local ownership – if the confusion of faith systems and half-commercial offers of a better way of life do not lead back into the old heresy-traps and make life and belief lop-sided, and if power politics do not get in the way.

Notes

Preface

1   Augustine, *De haeresibus ad Quodvultdeum*, 7, CCSL, 46, p.289.
2   Isidore, *Etymologiae*, ed. W. M. Lindsay (Oxford University Press, Oxford, 1911), VIII.1.
3   P. A. C. Vega, 'El "Liber de haeresibus" de San Isidoro de Sevilla y el "Codice Ovetense"', *La Cuidad de Dios*, clxxi (1958), 241–70.
4   Isidorus Hispalensis, *De haeresibus liber*, ed. P. A. C. Vega (El Escorial, 1940), p.25.
5   Ibid.
6   Isidore, *Etymologiae*, VIII.1.
7   *'Nulla est enim haeresis quae non ab aliis haereticis impugnetur, nulla philosophiae secularis secta quae ab aliis aeque stulta philosophiae sectis mendacii redarguatur'*, Bede, *In principium Genesis*, xi.8.9, CCSL, 118A, p.161.
8   Letter 2. *The Letters of John Hus*, trans. Matthew Spinka (Manchester University Press, Manchester, 1972), p.7.
9   Leslie Brubaker and John Haldon (eds) *Byzantium in the Iconoclast Era (c.680–850); The Sources, an Annotated Survey* (Ashgate, Aldershot, 2001), p.233.
10 PL 210.307.

11 John Wyclif, *Purgatorium sectae Christi*, 1, *Polemical Works*, ed. R. Buddensieg (Wyclif Society, London, 1883), 2 vols, vol. II, p.298.

12 John Wyclif, *De diabolo et membris eius*, 1, *Polemical Works*, vol. II, p.362.

13 Jan Hus, *De libris hereticorum legendis, Polemica*, ed. J. Ersil, *Opera Omnia*, 22 (In Aedibus Academiae Scientiarum Bohemoslovac, Prague, 1966), pp.19–37, p.21.

14 Ibid, p.30.

15 Ibid., pp.30–1.

Chapter 1 The Importance of Being United

1 Filastrius Brixiensis, *Diversarum hereseon liber*, CCSL, 9, p.217.

2 F. Schleiermacher, *The Christian Faith* (T and T Clark, Edinburgh, 1999), p.95.

3 Ibid., p.97.

4 Ibid.

5 Walter L. Wakefield and Austin P. Evans (eds) *Heresies of the High Middle Ages* (Columbia University Press, New York, 1969, reissued 1991), pp.173–85.

6 Wyclif, *De Nova Prevaricancia Mandatorum*, 1, *Polemical Works*, ed. R. Buddensieg (Wyclif Society, London, 1883), 2 vols, vol. II, p.116.

7 Ibid., 3, *Polemical Works*, vol. II, pp.122–4.

8 Ibid., *De Nova Prevaricancia Mandatorum*, 1, *Polemical Works*, vol. II, p.116.

9 John Hus, *De Libris Hereticorum Legendis, Polemica*, ed. J. Ersil, *Opera Omnia*, 22 (In Aedibus Academiae Scientiarum Bohemoslovac, Prague, 1966), pp.19–37, p.31.

10 Norman P. Tanner (ed.) *Decrees of the Ecumenical Councils* (Sheed and Ward, London/Georgetown University Press, Washington, 1990), vol. I, p.83.

11 Ibid., p.87.

12   Translation from H. J. D. Denzinger, *The Sources of Catholic Dogma*, quoted in Edward Peters (ed.) *Heresy and Authority in Mediaeval Europe* (University of Pennsylvania, Philadelphia, 1980), p.72.

13   PL 204.801.

14   Ibid., 204.805, 806, 822, 825.

15   Wyclif, *Sermones, Super Evangelia Dominicalia, Sermo* VI, ed. J. Loserth (Wyclif Society, London, 1887), vol. I, p.42; Wyclif, *Veritate Sacrae Scripturae*, ed. R. Buddensieg, vol.2 (Wyclif Society, London, 1905–6), 2 vols., vol.1, p.384.

16   Durandus de Huesca, *Une Somme anti-Cathare: le Liber Contra Manicheos*, ed. C. Thouzellier, *Spicilegium Sacrum Lovaniense*, 32 (Louvain University, Louvain, 1964), pp.95.

17   Ibid., p.106. On the Waldensians, see chapter 5.

18   Ibid., p.107.

19   *English Wycliffite Sermons*, ed. Anne Hudson and Pamela Gradon (Oxford University Press, Oxford, 1983–96), 5 vols., vol.4, p.114.

20   Ibid., p.115.

21   Ibid., pp.115–17.

22   Wyclif, *De fundatione sectarum, Polemical Works*, vol. I, p.74.

23   Ibid., p.75.

24   Wyclif, *De Veritate Sacrae Scripturae*.

25   Ibid., vol.1, p.382.

26   Ibid., *De Fundatione Sectarum*, vol. I, p.74.

27   Durandus de Huesca, *Une Somme anti-Cathare*, p.137.

28   Ibid., p.141.

29   See E. Montet, *Histoire litteraire des Vaudois du Piémont* (Paris 1885), p.192.

30   Wyclif, *Sermones, Super Evangelia Dominicalia*, vol. I, p.v.

31   Wyclif, *Opus Evangelicum*, ed. J. Loserth (Wyclif Society, London, 1895), 4 vols., vols I-II, p.37.

32   Ibid., p.368.

33   Ibid.

34   John Hus, *De Libris Hereticorum Legendis, Polemica*, p.35.

35   Wyclif, *Sermones, Super Evangelia Dominicalia, Sermo* 1, vol. I, pp.2–3.

Chapter 2 The Boundaries of Orthodoxy: Faith

1 The classic study on these matters remains J. N. D. Kelly, *Early Christian Creeds* (Longman, London, 1950 and subsequent editions). See, too, Gerd Lüdemann, *Heretics*, trans. John Bowden (SPCK, London, 1996).

2 Rufinus, *Commentarium in Symbolum Apostolorum*, 1, CCSL 20, p.134 ff. and translation in Kelly, *Early Christian Creeds*, pp.1–2.

3 Ignatius of Antioch, S*myrneans* 3.1ff; *Ephesians* 7.2, 18.2; *Magnesians* 11; *Trallians* 9.1 ff; *Smyrneans*.1.1 ff, *Works, The Apostolic Fathers*, ed. J. B. Lightfoot (Macmillan, London, 1869–85), vol.1.

4 Justin Martyr, *Apologia* (New York, Paulist Press, 1997), 26.6.

5 Faith and Order Paper no.153 (World Council of Churches, Geneva, 1991).

6 John Henry Newman, *Letters and Diaries*, XI (Oxford University Press, Oxford, 1961), p.63 and cf. p.71.

7 Ibid., p.27.

8 William Chillingworth, *Works* (Oxford University Press, Oxford, 1838), 3 vols., vol. II, p.386.

9 Newman, *Essay on the Development of Christian Doctrine* (University of Notre Dame Press, Notre Dame, IN [1878] 1989), p.3.

10 Cited in Owen Chadwick, *Bossuet to Newman* (Cambridge University Press, Cambridge, 1987), p.2.

Chapter 3 The Boundaries of Orthodoxy: Order

1 S. N. Eisenstadt, Reuven Kahane and David Shulman (eds) O*rthodoxy, Heterodoxy and Dissent in India* (Mouton, Berlin, 1984).

2 Robert E. Lerner, *The Heresy of the Free Spirit in the later Middle Ages* (University of California Press, Berkeley, 1972), pp.20–5.

3 Walter L. Wakefield and Austin P. Evans (eds) *Heresies of the High Middle Ages* (Columbia University Press, New York, 1969, reissued 1991), p.20.

4   Peter Godman, *Poetry of the Carolingian Renaissance* (Duckworth, London, 1985), pp.264–74.

5   Wyclif, *De Solutione Satane, Polemical Works*, ed. R. Buddensieg (Wyclif Society, London, 1883), vol. II.

6   Letter 30.ii.2, CCSL 4, p.200.

7   CCSL 4, p.137.

8   Letters, 17.i.1, CCCSL 3, p.96–7.

9   *On the Unity of the Catholic Church*, 7, CCSL 3, p.254.

10 Ibid., 6, CCSL 3, p.253.

11 Optatus of Milevis, Contra Donatistas, I.i.1, ed. M. Labrousse, *Sources chrétiennes*, 413 (Cerf, Paris, 1995–6), 2 vols., I, p.173.

12 Ibid., p.174.

13 Ibid., p.217.

14 Augustine, *Contra epistolam Parmeniani*, I.II.i.1–2, CSEL, 51 (1908), pp.98–9.

15 Ignatius of Antioch, 1 *Ephesians* 5.2–3; 20.1, I *Magnesians* 4.1, *Works, The Apostolic Fathers*, ed. J. B. Lightfoot (Macmillan, London, 1869–85), vol.1.

16 Letter 16, to the people of Louny, *The Letters of John Hus*, trans. Matthew Spinka (Manchester University Press, Manchester, 1972), p.49.

17 Letter 33, to Christian of Prachatice. *The Letters of John Hus*, p.94.

18 See Maximus the Confessor, *Selected Writings*, trans. George C. Berthold, *Classics of Western Spirituality* (Paulist Press, New York, 1985).

19 Craig L. Nessan, *Orthopraxis or Heresy: The North American Theological Response to Latin American Liberation Theology* (Scholars Press, Atlanta, GA, 1989).

Chapter 4   Classifying Heresies

1   C. Kannengiesser, *Arius and Athanasius* (Variorum, Basingstoke, 1991), p.1.

2   Arnobius, *Contre les gentils* (Belles Lettres, Paris, 1982), p.68.

3 Augustine, *De Haeresibus ad Quodvultdeum*, 5, CCSL, 46, p.288.

4 Ibid., *Retractions*, I.vii, CCSL 56, p.18.

5 *'Idem latine secta quod heresis graece significet'*, Bede, on Acts, 24.14, CCSL 121, p.90.

6 Augustine, *De Fide Rerum Invisibilium*, 10, CCSL 46 (1969).

7 Gregory of Tours, *Historiarum*, III.31, Monumenta Germanae Historica Scripture Rerum Merovingicarum 1, 2, ed. B. Krusch and W. Levison (Hahn, Hanover, 1965), p.127.

8 Bede, *On Luke*, 6.24, ed. D. Hurst, CCSL 120 (1960).

9 PL 39.1623.

10 Orosius, *Historiarum adversus paganos*, II, Book 6.i.5, ed. C. Zangmeister, CSEL, 5 (1868).

11 Isidore, *De differentiis verborum*, 282, PL 83.

12 Wyclif, *De Defectione perfidiarum Antichristi, Polemical Works*, ed. R. Buddensieg (Wyclif Society, London, 1883), vol. II, p.380.

13 There is a useful bringing together of these points in Thomas Renna, 'Wyclif's attacks on the monks', in *From Ockham to Wyclif. Studies in Church History, Subsidia*, 5, ed. Anne Hudson and Michael Wilks (Blackwell, Oxford, 1987), pp.267–80.

14 Wyclif, *De Fundatione Sectarum, Polemical Works*, vol. I, p.21.

15 Justin Martyr, *Apologia* (New York, Paulist Press, 1997), 1.26.

16 Isidore, *Etymologiae*, ed. W. M. Lindsay (Oxford, 1911), VIII.v.

17 Filastrius Brixiensis, *Diversarum Hereseon Liber*, LXVI, LXVII, CCSL, 9.

18 *Historia Ecclesiastica Tripartita*, ed. W. Jacob and R. Hanslik, I, 12, CSEL, 71 (Vienna, 1952), p.43; see also Eusebius/ Epiphanius/Cassiodorus, *Historia Tripartita*, ed. Walter Jacob and Rudolf Hanslik, CSEL (Berlin, 1954).

19 *Historia Ecclesiastica Tripartita*, ed. W. Jacob and R. Hanslik, I, 12, CSEL, 71 (Vienna, 1952), p.44.

20 Ibid., p.46.

21 Ibid., p.47.

22 Rowan Williams, *Arius: Heresy and Tradition* (Darton, Longman and Todd, London, 1987), p.83.

23 Norman P. Tanner (ed.) *Decrees of the Ecumenical Councils* (Sheed and Ward, London/Georgetown University Press, Washington, 1990), vol I., pp.16–17.

24 Williams, *Arius*, p.83.

25 *De symbolo*, I.ix.6, CCSL 60, p.326.

26 Peter the Venerable, *Contra petrobrusianos hereticos*, ed. J. Fearns, Corpus Christianorum Continuatio Medievalis (Brepols, Turnhout, 1968), 10, p.3.

27 Walter L. Wakefield and Austin P. Evans (eds) *Heresies of the High Middle Ages* (Columbia University Press, New York, 1969, reissued 1991), pp.254–5.

28 John M. Fletcher, 'Inter-faculty disputes in late mediaeval Oxford', in Hudson and Wilks (eds) *From Ockham to Wyclif*, pp.331–42.

29 A. Piepkorn, *Profiles in Belief* (Harper Row, New York, 1977–9), 3 vols., vol.2, p.3.

30 Letter 221, Augustine, *De Haeresibus ad Quodvultdeum*. CCSL, 46, p.273.

31 Letter 222, Ibid., p.277.

32 Filastrius Brixiensis, *Diversarum Hereseon Liber*. CCSL, 9, p.228 ff.

33 Ibid., p.217.

34 Augustine, *De Haeresibus ad Quodvultdeum*, 5, CCSL, 46, p.288.

35 *Patrologia Graeca* (J. P. Migne, Paris, 1979), 94.677–780.

36 Wakefield and Evans, *Heresies of the High Middle Ages*, p.103.

37 Durandus de Huesca, *Une Somme anti-Cathare: le Liber Contra Manicheos*, ed. C. Thouzellier, *Spicilegium Sacrum Lovaniense*, 32 (Louvain University, Louvain, 1964), p.82.

38 Bernard Gui, *Manuel de l'Inquisiteur*, ed. G. Mollat (Champion, Paris, 1926–7), 2 vols., vol.1, p.8.

39 *La registre d'inquisition de Jacques Fournier*, ed. J. Duvernoy (Bibliothèque méridionale, Toulouse, 1965), 3 vols., 41i, p.45.

40 Ibid., pp.46–7.

41 Prepositinus of Cremona, *Summa Contra Haereticos*, ed. J. N. Garvin and J. A. Corbett (Notre Dame University Press, Notre Dame, IN, 1958).

42 Robert Pattison, *The Great Dissent: John Henry Newman and the Liberal Heresy* (Oxford University Press, Oxford, 1991), p.57.

43 Matthew Spinka, *John Hus, a Biography* (Princeton University Press, Princeton, NJ, 1968), p.63–5. Letter 2. *The Letters of John Hus*, trans. Matthew Spinka (Manchester University Press, Manchester, 1972), p.3.

Chapter 5 Heresy and Social Challenge

1 Wyclif, *Sermones, Super Evangelia Dominicalia*, Sermo III, ed. J. Loserth (Wyclif Society, London, 1887), vol. I, p.24.

2 Letter 2, *The Letters of John Hus*, tr. Matthew Spinka (Manchester University Press, Manchester, 1972), p.7.

3 See the list in Walter L. Wakefield and Austin P. Evans, *Heresies of the High Middle Ages* (Columbia University Press, New York, 1991), p.20.

4 '*Omnis apostolica et evangelica institutio huiusmodi fine claudatur'*, PL 142.1271–1312, col. 1271–2.

5 Walter L. Wakefield and Austin P. Evans (eds) *Heresies of the High Middle Ages* (Columbia University Press, New York, 1969, reissued 1991), pp.189–94.

6 Ibid.

7 Ibid., p.97.

8 Wyclif, *De duobus generibus hereticorum, Polemical Works*, ed. R. Buddensieg (Wyclif Society, London, 1883), 2 vols., vol. II, pp.431–2.

9 On attitudes to penance, see E. Montet, *Histoire litteraire des Vaudois du Piémont* (Paris, 1885), p.192.

10 A. Dondaine, 'Aux origins du Valdéisme: une profession de foi de Valdès', *Archivum Fratrum Praedicatorum*, 16 (1946), 191–235, p.191.

11 Ibid., p.196.

12 Ibid., p.198.

13 Innocent III, Letters XI, 196, 18 December 1208, PL 215.1512, and Durandus de Huesca, *Une Somme anti-Cathare: le Liber Contra*

Manicheos, ed. C. Thouzellier, *Spicilegium Sacrum Lovaniense*, 32 (Louvain University, Louvain, 1964), pp.33 ff.

14 PL 216.1512–3.

15 C. Thouzellier, 'La profession trinitaire du Vaudois Durand de Huesca', *Récherches De théologie ancienne et médiévale*, 27 (1960), 267–289.

16 Dondaine, 'Aux origins du Valdéisme: une profession de foi de Valdès', pp.231–2.

17 Norman P. Tanner (ed.) *Decrees of the Ecumenical Councils* (Sheed and Ward, London/Georgetown University Press, Washington, 1990), vol. I, p.206, and see Walter Map, *De Nugis Curialium*, 1.31, ed. M. James, C. Brooke, R. Mynors (Oxford University Press, Oxford, 1983), 125–9.

18 Dondaine, 'Aux origins de Valdéisme'.

19 Tanner, *Decrees of the Ecumenical Councils*, vol. I, p.234.

20 See for example, Simon Tugwell, 'Notes on the Life of St. Dominic', *Archivum Fratrum Praedicatorum*, 178 (1998), 1–116, p.66.

21 PL 210.377–88.

22 G. Audisio, *The Waldensian Dissent* (Cambridge University Press, Cambridge, 1999), p.33.

23 Dondaine, 'Aux origins du Valdéisme', p.197.

24 Audisio, *The Waldensian Dissent*, p.28.

25 John M. Fletcher, 'Inter-faculty disputes in late mediaeval Oxford', in *From Ockham to Wyclif. Studies in Church History, Subsidia, 5*, ed. Anne Hudson and Michael Wilks (Blackwell, Oxford, 1987), pp.331–42.

26 A. K. McHardy, 'The dissemination of Wyclif's ideas', in Hudson and Wilks, *From Ockham to Wyclif*, pp.361–8.

27 A. Kenny, *Wyclif* (Oxford University Press, Oxford, 1985), p.65.

28 On all this, see Matthew Spinka, *John Hus' Concept of the Church* (Princeton University Press, Princeton, NJ, 1966).

29 Letter 1, *The Letters of John Hus*, p.2.

30 Howard Kaminsky, *A History of the Hussite Revolution* (University of California Press, Berkeley and Los Angeles, 1967), p.23.

31   Matthew Spinka, *John Hus, a Biography* (Princeton University Press, Princeton, NJ, 1968), p.63–5.

32   Letter 7, to Archbishop Zbynek, *The Letters of John Hus*, p.22.

33   *Historické spisy Petra z Mladonovic a jine z právy a mameti o M. Janovi Husovi a M. Jeronymovi z prahy*, ed. V. Novotny, *Fontes rerum Bohemicarum* (Prague, 1932), VIII, 25–120, citing Peter of Mladonovice, 'An account of the trial and condemnation of Master John Hus in Constance', English text in Matthew Spinka, *John Hus at the Council of Constance* (Columbia University Press, New York/London,1965).

34   Peter of Mladonovice, 'An account of the trial and condemnation of Master John Hus in Constance', English text in Matthew Spinka, *John Hus at the Council of Constance* (Columbia University Press, New York/London,1965), p.99.

35   Spinka, *John Hus at the Council of Constance*.

36   Ibid., p.112.

37   Ibid., p.113.

38   Ibid., p.81.

39   Ibid., p.91.

40   Ibid., p.125.

41   Ibid., p.170.

42   Letter 27, to the people of Prague, *The Letters of John Hus*, p.84.

43   Kaminsky, *A History of the Hussite Revolution*, p.95.

44   Letter 34, to Christian of Prachatice, *The Letters of John Hus*, p.96.

45   Ibid., p.99.

46   Ibid., p.96.

47   Letter 31, to the lords gathered at the supreme court of the Kingdom of Bohemia, *The Letters of John Hus*, p.90.

48   Kaminsky, *A History of the Hussite Revolution*, pp.97–8.

49   On the Taborites and other manifestations of the Hussite movement, see Kaminsky, *A History of the Hussite Revolution*, pp.311 ff.

50   Keith Hampson, '"God and Mammon": Religious protest and educational change in New England from the revolution to

the Golden Age', in *Studies in Church History*, 9, ed. Derek Baker (Cambridge University Press, Cambridge, 1972), 351–65, p.352.

51 Ibid., p.358.

52 Wyclif, *Sermones*, vol. I, p.v.

Chapter 6   Good and Evil

1 Bede on Luke, VI.xxiv.37, CCSL 120ii, p.418.

2 Bede, *In principium Genesis*, CCSL, 118.

3 Walter L. Wakefield and Austin P. Evans (eds) *Heresies of the High Middle Ages* (Columbia University Press, New York, 1969, reissued 1991), p.450.

4 *Patrologia Graeca*, 100.501.

5 Wakefield and Evans, *Heresies of the High Middle Ages*, pp.248–9.

6 Bernard Gui, *Manuel de l'Inquisiteur*, ed. G. Mollat (Champion, Paris, 1926–7), 2 vols., vol.1, p.10.

7 Wakefield and Austin, *Heresies of the High Middle Ages*, p.332.

8 Ibid., p.523.

9 Ibid., p.543.

10 Ibid., p.627.

11 Bernard Hamilton, 'The Cathars and Christian perfection', in *The Medieval Church: Universities, Heresy and the Religious Life. Essays in Honour of Gordon Leff*, Studies in Church History, Subsidia, *11*, ed. Peter Biller and Barrie Dobson (Boydell and Brewer, Woodbridge, 1999), pp.5–23.

12 *La registre d'inquisition de Jacques Fournier*, ed. J. Duvernoy (Bibliothèque méridionale, Toulouse, 1965), 3 vols., vol.41i, p.282.

13 Ibid., p.281.

14 Ibid., pp.282–3.

15 Ibid., p.18.

16 Wakefield and Austin, *Heresies of the High Middle Ages*, pp.254–5.

1   Bernard of Clairvaux, In Cant. 64.iii.8, *Opera Omnia*, 2, ed. J. Leclercq, H. M. Rochais and C. H. Talbot (Editiones Cistercienses, Rome, 1958), p.170.

2   Aquinas, *Summa contra Gentiles*, ed. C. Pera (Vatican, Rome, 1961), 3 vols.

3   Wyclif, *Opus Evangelicum*, ed. J. Loserth (Wyclif Society, London, 1895), 4 vols., vols I-II, p.2.

4   Ibid., p.3.

5   Kurt Villads Jensen, 'Robert Holcot's Questio on killing infidels: an evaluation and an edition', *Archivum Fratrum Praedicatorum*, 63 (1993), 207–28.

6   Norman P. Tanner (ed.) *Decrees of the Ecumenical Councils* (Sheed and Ward, London/Georgetown University Press, Washington, 1990), vol.1, pp.233–4.

7   PL 204.777.

8   Letter 9, *The Letters of John Hus*, trans. Matthew Spinka (Manchester University Press, Manchester, 1972), p.35–6.

9   *La Registre d'Inquisition de Jacques Fournier*, ed. J. Duvernoy (Bibliothèque méridionale, Toulouse, 1965), 3 vols., vol.41i, p.274.

10   Ibid., p.201.

11   Bernard Gui, *Manuel de l'Inquisiteur*, ed. G. Mollat (Champion, Paris, 1926–7), 2 vols., vol.1, p.26.

12   *La Registre d'Inquisition de Jacques Fournier*.

13   Ibid., p.123.

14   Ibid., p.173.

15   Bernard Gui, *Manuel de l'Inquisiteur*.

16   Tanner, *Decrees of the Ecumenical Councils*, vol.1, pp.380–2.

17   Ibid., pp.382–3.

18   Bernard Gui, *Manuel de l'Inquisiteur*, vol.1, p.xvi.

19   Ibid., pp.4–6.

20   Wyclif, *Sermones*, *Super Evangelia Dominicalia*, Sermo I, ed. J. Loserth (Wyclif Society, London, 1887), vol. I, p.2.

21   Ibid., Sermo III, vol. I, p.17.

22   Ibid., p.18.

23   Ibid., p.20.

24   Wyclif, *De Fundatione Sectarum, Polemical Works*, ed. R. Buddensieg (Wyclif Society, London, 1883), 2 vols., vol. I, p.74.

25   Wyclif, *Opus Evangelicum*, vols I-II, pp.18–9.

26   Wyclif, *De Citationibus Frivolis, Polemical Works*, vol. I, p.74., vol.2, p.552.

27   Bernard Williams, 'Tolerating the intolerable', in *The Politics of Toleration in Modern Life*, ed. Susan Mendus (Duke University Press, Durham, NC/ Edinburgh University Press, Edinburgh, 1999), p.74.

28   William Chillingworth, *Works* (Oxford University Press, Oxford, 1838), 3 vols., vol. I, pp.112–3.

29   Ibid., vol. II, p.330.

30   Milton, *Areopagitica*, in *Complete Prose Works*, ed. Don M. Wolfe (Yale University Press, New Haven, CT, 1953–82), vol.2, p.519–20.

31   John Locke, *A Letter Concerning Toleration*, ed. J. Horton and Susan Mendus (Routledge, London, 1991), p.47.

32   Ibid., p.12.

33   Ibid., p.14.

34   Ibid., p.20.

35   Ibid., p.14.

36   Ibid., p.23.

37   Ibid., p.24.

38   Ibid., p.25.

39   Ibid., pp.17–18.

40   Ibid., p.19.

41   Ibid., p.43.

42   Karl Rahner, *On Heresy* (Burn and Oates, London, 1964), p.55.

Conclusion

1 PL 214. 921
2 Walter L. Wakefield and Austin P. Evans (eds) *Heresies of the High Middle Ages* (Columbia University Press, New York, 1969, reissued 1991), p.186.
3 Robert F. Barsky, *Noam Chomsky: A Life of Dissent* (MIT Press, Cambridge, MA, 1997), p.122.
4 Ibid., pp.162,165.
5 Ibid., pp.176–7.
6 Ambrose Bierce, *Skepticism and Dissent: Selected Journalism 1889–1901*, 25 April 1901, ed. Lawrence I. Berkove (UMI Research Press, Ann Arbor, MI, 1986–90).
7 Ibid., 26 November 1899, p.170.
8 Letter 7, to Archbishop Zbynek. *The Letters of John Hus*, trans. Matthew Spinka (Manchester University Press, Manchester, 1972), p.22.
9 Ibid.

Abbreviations used in Notes and References

CCCM *Corpus Christianorum Continuatio Medievalis*, Brepols, Turnhout, 1953–
CCSL *Corpus Christianorum Series Latina*, Brepols, Turnhout, 1953–
CSEL *Corpus Scriptorum Ecclesiasticorum Latinorum*, Vienna, 1866–
PL *Patrologia Latina*, Paris, 1864–

Further Reading

General Reference

Encyclopaedia of Early Christianity, 2nd edn., ed. Everett Ferguson (Garland, New York/London, 1997).
A New Dictionary of Christian Theology, ed. Alan Richardson and John Bowden (SCM, London, 1983).
The Oxford Dictionary of the Christian Church, ed. F. L. Cross and E. A. Livingstone (Oxford University Press, Oxford, 2002).
The Westminster Dictionary of Church History, ed. Jerald C. Braver (Westminster Press, Philadelphia, 1971).

Sources

Aquinas, Thomas, *Summa contra Gentiles*, ed. C. Pera (Vatican, Rome, 1961), 3 vols.
Arnobius, *Contre les gentiles* (Belles Lettres, Paris, 1982).
Augustine, *De haeresibus ad Quodvultdeum*, 7, CCSL, 46.
Augustine, *Contra epistolam Parmeniani*, CSEL, 51 (1908).
Bede, *In Principium Genesis*, CCSL 118.
Bernard Gui, *Manuel de l'Inquisiteur*, ed. G. Mollat (Champion, Paris, 1926–7).

Bierce, Ambrose, *Skepticism and Dissent: Selected Journalism 1889–1901*, ed. Lawrence I. Berkove (UMI Research Press, Ann Arbor, MI, 1986–90).

Cyprian, *Opera*, CCSL 3.

Durandus de Huesca, *Une Somme anti-Cathare: le Liber Contra Manicheos*, ed. C. Thouzellier, *Spicilegium Sacrum Lovaniense*, 32 (1964).

Duvernoy, J. (ed.), *La registre d'inquisition de Jacques Fournier* (Bibliothèque méridionale, Toulouse, 1965), 3 vols.

Filastrius Brixiensis, *Diversarum hereseon liber*, CCSL, 9.

Gregory of Tours, *Historiarum*, ed. B. Krusch and W. Levison Monumenta Germanae Historica Scripture Rerum Merovingicarum 1, 2, (Hahn, Hanover, 1965).

Hermannus Judaeus, *De conversione sua*, ed. G. Niemeyer (Monumenta Germanae Historica, Weimar, 1967).

Hudson, Anne and Gradon, Pamela, *English Wycliffite Sermons* (Oxford University Press, Oxford, 1983–96), 5 vols.

Hus, Jan, *Opera Omnia* (In Aedibus Academiae Scientiarum Bohemoslovac, Prague, 1966).

Hus, Jan, *The Letters of John Hus*, trans. Matthew Spinka (Manchester University Press, Manchester, [1920] 1972).

Ignatius of Antioch, *Works, The Apostolic Fathers*, ed. J. B. Lightfoot (Macmillan, London, 1869–85), vol.1.

Isidore, *De haeresibus liber*, ed. P. A. C. Vega (El Escorial, 1940).

Isidore, *Etymologiae*, ed. W. M. Lindsay (Oxford University Press, Oxford, 1911), 2 vols.

Isidore, *Liber de variis quaestionibus adversus Judaeos seu ceteros infideles . . . ex utroque Testamento collectus*, ed. P. A. C. Vega and A. E. Anspach (El Escorial, 1940).

Jacob, W. and R. Hanslik *Historia Ecclesiastica Tripartita*, I, 12, CSEL, 71 (Vienna, 1952).

Locke, John, *A Letter Concerning Toleration*, ed. J. Horton and Susan Mendus (Routledge, London, 1991).

Maximus the Confessor, *Selected Writings*, trans. George C. Berthold, *Classics of Western Spirituality* (Paulist Press, New York, 1985).

Milton, *Areopagitica*, in *Complete Prose Works*, ed. Don M. Wolfe (Yale University Press, New Haven, CT, 1953–82), vol 2.

Newman, John Henry, *Letters and Diaries* (Oxford University Press, Oxford, 1984).

Novatian, *Opera*, ed. G. F.Diercks, CCSL, 4 (1972).

Optatus of Milevis, *Contra Donatistas*, ed. M. Labrousse, *Sources chrétiennes*, 413 (Cerf, Paris, 1995–6).

Peter the Venerable, *Contra Petrobrusianos Hereticos*, ed. J. Fearns, CCCM (Brepols, Turnhout, 1968), 10.

Rahner, Karl, *On Heresy* (Burn and Oates, London, 1964).

Rufinus, *Commentarium in Symbolum Apostolorum*, 1, CCSL 20.

Tanner, Norman P. (ed.) *Decrees of the Ecumenical Councils* (Sheed and Ward, London/Georgetown University Press, Washington, DC, 1990), 2 vols.

Walter Map, *De Nugis Curialium*, 1.31, ed. M. James, C. Brooke and R. Mynors (Oxford University Press, Oxford, 1983).

Wyclif, John *Latin Works* (Wyclif Society, London, 1883–97).

Secondary Literature

Audisio, Gabriel, *The Waldensian Dissent, Persecution and Survival c.1170-c.1570*, trans. C. Davison (Cambridge University Press, Cambridge, 1989).

Audisio, G. *The Waldensian Dissent* (Cambridge University Press, Cambridge, 1999).

Barber, M., *The Cathars* (Pearson, Harlow, 2000).

Barsky, Robert F., *Noam Chomsky: A Life of Dissent* (MIT Press, Cambridge, MA, 1997).

Berger, Peter L., *The Heretical Imperative* (Collins, London, 1980).

Brubaker, L. and Haldon, J. (eds) *Byzantium in the Iconoclast Era (c.680–850); The Sources, an Annotated Survey* (Ashgate, Aldershot, 2001).

Chadwick, Owen, *Bossuet to Newman* (Cambridge University Press, Cambridge, 1987).

Dondaine, A., 'Aux origins du Valdéisme: une profession de foi de Valdès', *Archivum Fratrum Praedicatorum*, 16 (1946), 191–235.

Eisenstadt, S. N., Kahane, Reuven and Shulman, David (eds) *Orthodoxy, Heterodoxy and Dissent in India* (Mouton, Berlin, New York, Amsterdam, 1984).

Fletcher, John M., 'Inter-faculty disputes in late mediaeval Oxford' in *From Ockham to Wyclif. Studies in Church History, Subsidia, 5*, ed. Anne Hudson and Michael Wilks (Blackwell, Oxford, 1987), pp.331–42.

Godman, Peter, *Poetry of the Carolingian Renaissance* (Duckworth, London, 1985), pp.264–74.

Grant, Robert M., *Heresy and Criticism: The Search for Authenticity in Early Christian Literature* (Westminster/John Knox Press, Louisville, KY, 1993).

Guy, John, 'Perceptions of heresy, 1200–1550' in *Reformation, Humanism and "Revolution"*, ed. G. J. Schocher (Folger Institute, Washington, DC, 1990), pp.39–61.

Hamilton, Bernard,'The Cathars and Christian perfection', in *The Medieval Church: Universities, Heresy and the Religious Life. Essays in Honour of Gordon Leff*, ed. Peter Biller and Barrie Dobson, *Studies in Church History, Subsidia, 11* (Boydell and Brewer, Woodbridge, 1999), pp.5–23.

Hamilton, J. and Hamilton, B., *Christian Dualist Heresies in the Byzantine world, c.650–1450* (Manchester University Press, Manchester, 1998).

Hampson, Keith, '"God and Mammon": Religious protest and educational change in New England from the revolution to the Golden Age', in *Studies in Church History, 9*, ed. Derek Baker (Cambridge University Press, Canmbridge, 1972), pp.351–65.

Hudson, A., *The Premature Reformation* (Oxford University Press, Oxford, 1988).

Hudson, A, and Gradon, P., *English Wycliffite Writings* (Cambridge University Press, Cambridge, 1978).

Hudson, Anne and Wilks, Michael (eds), *From Ockham to Wyclif, Studies in Church History, Subsidia, 5* (Blackwell, Oxford, 1987).

Jensen, Kurt Villads,'Robert Holcot's Questio on killing infidels: an evaluation and an edition', *Archivum Fratrum Praedicatorum, 63* (1993), 207–228.

Kaminsky, Howard, *A History of the Hussite Revolution* (University of California Press, Berkeley and Los Angeles, 1967).

Kannengiesser, C, *Arius and Athanasius* (Variorum, Basingstoke, 1991).

Kelly, J. N. D., *Early Christian Creeds* (Longman, London, 1950 and subsequent editions).

Kenny, A., *Wyclif* (Oxford University Press, Oxford, 1985).

Kenny, A., *Wyclif in his Times* (Oxford University Press, Oxford, 1986).

Lambert, Malcolm, *Medieval Heresy* (Blackwell, Oxford, 1992), 2nd edn.

Lerner, Robert E., 'The image of mixed liquids in late medieval mystical thought', *Church History*, 40 (1971), 397–411.

Lerner, Robert E., *The Heresy of the Free Spirit in the Later Middle Ages* (University of California Press, 1972), pp.20–25.

Lüdemann, Gerd, *Heretics*, trans. John Bowden (SPCK, London, 1996).

A. K. McHardy, 'The dissemination of Wyclif's ideas', in *From Ockham to Wyclif, Studies in Church History, Subsidia, 5* (Blackwell, Oxford, 1987), pp.361–8.

Montet, E., *Histoire litteraire des Vaudois du Piémont* (Gallimard, Paris, 1885).

Moore, R. I., *The Birth of Popular Heresy* (Edward Arnold, London, 1975).

Nessan, Craig L., *Orthopraxis or Heresy: The North American Theological Response to Latin American Liberation Theology* (Scholars Press, Atlanta, GA, 1989).

Greenshields, Malcolm R. and Robinson, Thomas A. (eds) *Orthodoxy and Heresy in Religious Movements: Discipline and Dissent* (Edwin Mellen, Lewiston, ME, 1992).

Peters, Edward (ed. and trans.), *Heresy and Authority in Mediaeval Europe* (Pennsylvania University Press, Philadelphia, 1980), p.72.

Piepkorn, A., *Profiles in Belief* (Harper Row, New York, 1977–9), 3 vols.

Robertson, E. H., *John Wycliffe: Morning Star of the Reformation* (Marshall, Basingstoke, 1984).

Robson, J. A., *Wyclif and the Oxford Schools* (Cambridge University Press, Cambridge, 1961).

Schleiermacher, F., *The Christian Faith* (T and T Clark, Edinburgh, 1999).

Spinka, M., *John Hus at the Council of Constance* (Columbia University Press, New York/London, 1965).

Spinka, M., *John Hus' Concept of the Church* (Princeton University Press, Princeton, NJ, 1966).

Spinka, Matthew, *John Hus, a Biography* (Princeton University Press, Princeton, NJ, 1968).

Stephens, Prescot, *The Waldensian Story* (Book Guild, Lewes, 1998).

Wakefield, Walter L. and Evans, Austin P. (eds), *Heresies of the High Middle Ages* (Columbia, New York, 1969, reissued 1991).

Walsh, K., *Richard Fitzralph in Oxford, Avignon and Armagh* (Oxford University Press, Oxford, 1981).

Williams, Rowan, *Arius: Heresy and Tradition* (Darton Longman and Todd, London, 1987).

World Council of Churches, *Confessing the one Faith: an Ecumenical Explication of the Apostolic Faith* (Faith and Order paper no.153, World Council of Churches, Geneva, 1991).

Index